PRAISE FOR
HARRY POTTER AND THE ART OF SPYING
YOUNG AGENT EDITION

"A truly imaginative romp through much of the spycraft I tried
to teach Harry—almost as pleasant as lemon drops!"

– ALBUS DUMBLEDORE

"Harry finally figured everything out—thanks to me. Maybe
he wouldn't have been so slow if he had this wonderful book."

– SEVERUS SNAPE

"A truly intellectual book to teach the younger reader
much of what we—well, at least what I—learned roaming
the stacks in the library."

– HERMIONE GRANGER

"A real giant of a book! But the *Monster Book of
Monsters* 'tweer better."

– RUBEUS HAGRID

★ YOUNG AGENT EDITION ★

# HARRY POTTER AND THE ART OF SPYING

## UNAUTHORIZED

**LYNN BOUGHEY**
AUTHOR OF THE SPY NOVEL, MISSION TO CHARA

**PETER EARNEST**
EXECUTIVE DIRECTOR, INTERNATIONAL SPY MUSEUM

**KEVIN CANNON**
ILLUSTRATOR

artofspying.net

WISE
CREATIVE • PUBLISHING
Ink

This book has not been approved, licensed, or sponsored by any entity or person
involved in creating or producing Harry Potter, the book series or films.Not
authorized by J. K. Rowling, Harry Potter Publishing Rights, Warner Bros.,or
related properties. The manuscript has been reviewed and cleared for public release
by the Department of Defense, Office of Security Review, DOPSR # 16-S-2824
(December 8, 2016) in relation to Lynn Boughey and by the CIA Publications
Review Board (November 29, 2016) in relation to Peter Earnest.

All statements of fact, opinion, or analysis expressed are those of the authors and
do not reflect the official positions or views of the Department of Defense, the
CIA, or any other U.S. Government agency. Nothing in the contents should be
construed as asserting or implying U.S. Government authentication of information
or endorsement of the authors' views. This material has been reviewed solely for
classification.

ISBN 13: 978-1-63489-045-8

Library of Congress Catalog Number: 2017930751

Printed in the United States of America
Third Printing: 2021
25   24   23   22   21          7   6   5   4   3

Illustrated by Kevin Cannon. Mazes by Maggie Hertz
Cover and Interior design and typesetting by James Monroe Design LLC.

Wise Ink, Inc. • www.wiseinkpub.com

Follow us on Facebook and our webpage artofspying.net

# CONTENTS

# ACTIVITY PAGES CONTENTS

## ACTIVITY ON THE FRONT FLAP

## ACTIVITIES AT THE END OF CHAPTER 1

# ACTIVITY PAGES CONTENTS

## ACTIVITIES AT THE END OF CHAPTER 2

## ACTIVITIES AT THE END OF CHAPTER 3

## ACTIVITIES AT THE END OF CHAPTER 4

## ACTIVITIES AT THE END OF CHAPTER 5

# ACTIVITY PAGES CONTENTS

## ACTIVITIES AT THE END OF CHAPTER 6

## ACTIVITY ON THE BACK FLAP

# ACKNOWLEDGMENTS

The authors gratefully acknowledge the following persons who were instrumental in the creation of this Young Agent Edition and our prior book.

Production was coordinated by Amy Quale of Wise Ink Creative Publishing, Minneapolis. Amy brought in Kevin Cannon of Minneapolis, our illustrator, and Jay Monroe of James Monroe Design of Duluth, Minnesota, who also did the set up for the initial volume, the original cover, and this cover. Both worked tirelessly in creating a wonderful design and artwork appropriate to the younger audience. And Kevin notes his thanks to Maggie Hertz for performing her magic on the mazes. We absolutely love the illustrations, the cover, and the look of the book, and we thank you both Kevin and Jay for all you did!

The initial editing, turning the initial book into a Young Adult version, was performed by Kellie Hultgren of KMH Editing; additional editing of the authors' final draft was performed by Molly Miller and Graham Warnken, as well as Amy Quale. We note, however, that any errors are ours alone.

Throughout this process we have had the advice and counsel of Allison Bishop of the International Spy Museum, along with great support from throughout the Spy Museum, especially the bookstore, including Mary Henderson, Peter's assistant.

Amy also managed the PR plan and was assisted by Roseanne Cheng. Social media set up was conducted by Gary Robson, and social media for our first book was performed Kelsey Neilson, *née* Roebuck, who kept the tweets and blogs current and interesting. She and her (now) husband Jake Neilson created our PowerPoint presentation, which was unveiled at LeakyCon 2014. We thank the Independent Book Publishers Association for awarding the initial book 1st Place nationally (Ben Franklin Award) in the category of Teen Nonfiction, and The Gelett Burgess Center for its 1st Place Children's Book Award in the category of Reference. We are also pleased to be finalists with our initial book in 2015 in regards to receiving two regional book awards, the High Plains Book Award and the Midwest Book Award.

Foremost of all, Lynn thanks Peter for joining him in this magical endeavor, combining the joy we have found in the Harry Potter series with our love of intelligence, tradecraft, and the people who serve our country in so many ways. Lynn also thanks his fourteen-year-old twin daughters, Miranda and Sophia, for being such a wonderful part of his life, as well as attending the book launch and many book signings.

Peter thanks Lynn for inviting him to join in this thoughtful study of J.K. Rowling's wonderful creation, Harry Potter, a story that continues to entrance children, young and old, throughout the world. And for our shared hope that this little book enhances the enjoyment of readers everywhere who share our love of Harry. Finally, he extends special thanks to his wife Karen Rice for serving as the "Hermione" in his own life, especially for her unfailing support, unquenchable joy for living, generosity of spirit, and love of adventure.

# BOOK REFERENCES
# USE OF INITIALS

Throughout this book we provide page references so the reader can review what was said or what happened in the original book. We sometimes employ the following abbreviations as to the seven books in the Harry Potter series.

**Book 1**    **SS**—*Harry Potter and the Sorcerer's Stone*

**Book 2**    **CS**—*Harry Potter and the Chamber of Secrets*

**Book 3**    **PA**—*Harry Potter and the Prisoner of Azkaban*

**Book 4**    **GF**—*Harry Potter and the Goblet of Fire*

**Book 5**    **OP**—*Harry Potter and the Order of the Phoenix*

**Book 6**    **HBP**—*Harry Potter and the Half-Blood Prince*

**Book 7**    **DH**—*Harry Potter and the Deathly Hallows*

# Chapter 1

## SPIES AMONG US

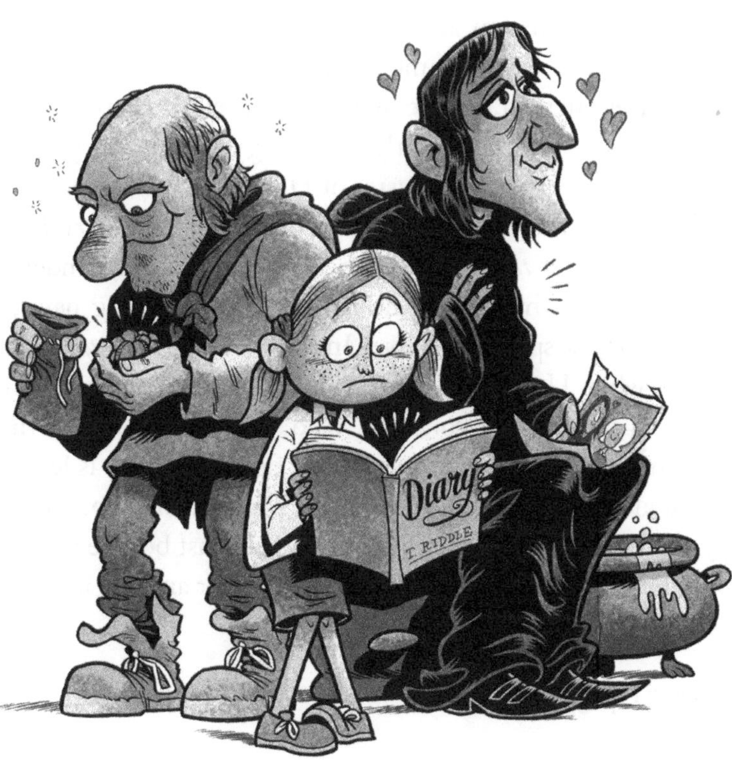
Diary
T. RIDDLE

Any fan of the Harry Potter series knows that the books are full of sneaking around, eavesdropping, clever disguises, and amazing gadgets—all things that we associate with the world of espionage. Harry's world is full of magical spells and devices that Muggles can only dream about, but the challenges he faces, as well as the skills he uses to defeat his archenemy, Voldemort, can teach us a lot about how spies operate in the modern world.

In the Muggle world, a spy is a person who secretly watches what other people do, especially someone who attempts to get secret information about one country for another country. Harry Potter fans will immediately think of Professor Severus Snape, the talented **double agent** who pretended to work for the Dark Lord while secretly reporting Voldemort's plans to Albus Dumbledore, headmaster of Hogwarts and leader of the Order of the Phoenix. But, at the beginning of *Harry Potter and the Order of the Phoenix,* when Harry is hiding under an open window while his uncle listens to the evening news, is Harry being a spy? Of course! In *Harry Potter and the Goblet of Fire,* when Hermione carefully analyzes the content of Rita Skeeter's articles and considers who was present at the time the comments were made in order to figure out who is leaking confidential information to the *Daily Prophet,* she, too, is doing spy work as an intelligence analyst. A spy must be able not only to gather information, but also to interpret or analyze it.

## TYPES OF SPIES

Because there are many different types of information to be collected, and many different situations in which to collect them, there are many different types of spies. When most people think of spies, they imagine someone like the fictional character James Bond, or the early American spy Nathan Hale, who snuck into enemy territory to spy on British troops during the Revolutionary War.

## NATHAN HALE

Nathan Hale was born in Connecticut in 1755. When the American colonists rose up against their British rulers, Hale left his job as a teacher to join his five brothers in the fight for independence. When General George Washington asked for a volunteer to cross enemy lines to spy on the British forces, Hale stepped up. Hale, pretending to be a Dutch schoolmaster, was captured by the British. The secret information he carried marked him as a spy—a crime punishable by death. His last words, before his execution by hanging on September 22, 1776, were said to have been, "I only regret that I have but one life to lose for my country." He was twenty-one years old.

~~~~~~~~~~~~~~~~~~~~~~~~~~~~~~~~~~~~~~~~~

Intelligence officers who work in the field—that is, in other countries—are called **case officers**. Case officers **recruit agents** to spy for their country. A case officer manages or "handles" the agent and directs his or her espionage activities. Harry's batty old cat-loving neighbor, Mrs. Figg, is secretly an agent or **mole** who keeps watch over Harry while he lives at number four, Privet Drive. Mrs. Figg's handler, as we learn in *Harry Potter and the Order of the Phoenix*, is Albus Dumbledore himself!

~~~~~~~~~~~~~~~~~~~~~~~~~~~~~~~~~~~~~~~~~

## AGENT VS. CASE OFFICER

Members of spy agencies who go out into the field and gather information (or recruit persons to spy or provide information to them) are normally called case officers, not *agents*. Agents are the people they recruit to spy for them. It should be noted that there are other types of intelligence officers, such as intelligence analysts who analyze the information obtained by case officers and from other collection systems. In addition, there are many persons who provide other types of support to intelligence operations, including scientists, psychologists, engineers, mathematicians, code-breakers and code-makers, and other people who provide assistance to complete the mission.

~~~~~~~~~~~~~~~~~~~~~~~~~~~~~~~~

Most intelligence officers work at desks, reading reports and using computers to analyze information. These "desk" intelligence officers are called *analysts*. They analyze the secret information covertly gathered by case officers and sort through other bits and pieces of public and secretly acquired information in order to do their analyses. The answers they seek might expose an adversary's secret plans, a country's financial and scientific strengths or weaknesses, or information about some new weapon.

~~~~~~~~~~~~~~~~~~~~~~~~~~~~~~~~

## PRIVATE EYES AND CORPORATE SPIES

Intelligence gathering isn't just governments spying on each other. Spying takes place inside countries as well, and even inside and between individual organizations. Corporations work hard to ensure that their competition doesn't **bribe** an employee to spill details about new products or secret formulas. There are intelligence professionals who specialize in corporate espionage, both preventing and using it. More recently hacking has become a major concern, for governments as well as private industry. And of course anyone in the private sector can pay a private investigator to do some spying for them, whether it's locating a runaway child or catching a cheating business partner. Local police departments have intelligence networks too, using information collected from officers, ordinary citizens, and **informants** to stop crimes before they take place. Good or bad, spies can be anywhere!

## MOTIVATION AND LOYALTY

Whether a spy is breaking into an adversary's wall safe or combing through Internet records in a distant office, there are two important factors that affect his or her work: *motivation* (the things that make that person want to be a spy) and *loyalty* (faithfulness). Before **recruiting** someone (asking them to become a spy), a good intelligence officer will work hard to understand that person's reasons for wanting to spy. A recruiter must ask: What are the individual motives of the person or persons I'm trying to recruit? Do they have a vendetta against me or my enemy? Have they indicated which side they are on? If they decide to remain neutral, can I still use them in some manner? A spy might work in return for money, or revenge, or the opportunity to serve a cause.

## OF MICE AND MEN—THE FOUR INCENTIVES TO SPY, OR MICE

In the spy world, we use the acronym MICE to list the four most common reasons to spy:

Money—Ideology—Coercion—Ego

After recruiting a spy, the intelligence officer will try to make sure that the person remains loyal to the officer's organization or country.

## SPYING FOR PERSONAL GAIN — MONEY

Some spies will work for money, such as Aldrich Ames, a **CIA** case officer to whom the Soviets offered over $2 million to spy for them. Personal gain is their motivation, and their loyalty is to whoever pays them the most. In the modern world, hiring a spy can be quite dangerous—because there's always the chance that your opponent will make your spy a better financial offer. If that person decides to switch sides or **"turn,"** he or she has information about you that can be used against you!

While most of the spies in the world of Harry Potter are working for patriotic or personal reasons, there is one person who always seems to be looking for personal gain: Mundungus Fletcher. While he seems like a good guy at heart, he can't pass up any good "business opportunity" that comes his way. His loyalty to the Order of the Phoenix wavers when he sees the chance for profit, such as when he leaves Harry unguarded in the beginning of *Harry Potter and the Order of the Phoenix*, and that makes him less than reliable as a spy. But as the Weasley brothers attest, Mundungus "hears things that we don't" (*OP* 86–87).

A better example in the Potter world of a character who spies for personal gain might be Peter Pettigrew; his desired "gain" is not money but power. Peter was a friend of James and Lily Potter, but at some point he decided that he would benefit more if he switched to Voldemort's side. When the Potters made Peter their Secret Keeper, he traded that information to Voldemort in return for promises of power and prestige under the Dark Lord's reign. Of course, things didn't go as planned for Voldemort, and Peter had to spend over a decade in hiding as a rat—not the reward he'd hoped to gain (but certainly one he well deserved)!

## SPYING FOR PATRIOTISM—IDEOLOGY

Many spies are motivated by the desire to serve their country. They feel that it is their patriotic duty to gather and analyze information in order to stop enemies from attacking or spying on their home country. Nathan Hale became a spy because he believed that the thirteen colonies in America should be free of British rule. He gave his loyalty to the Continental Army. More recently, hundreds of patriotic Americans joined the military and the CIA following 9-11.

In the world of Harry Potter, a good example of a patriotic spy is Professor Lupin—who spies on the werewolves, at great risk to himself. A less positive role model is Professor Umbridge. She believes that anything the Ministry of Magic does is absolutely right. She is completely loyal to the Ministry of Magic—even to the point of drugging students and torturing Harry ("I must not tell lies").

## TRAITOR OR HERO?

One famous patriotic spy from the Cold War between the United States and the Soviet Union was Colonel Ryszard Kuklinski, a Polish military officer who had **access** to Soviet battle plans. As an officer in the Polish Army, Kuklinski knew about the plan to march the Soviet army through Poland in order to attack countries in Western Europe. When he realized that those plans would make his home country a target in a potential nuclear exchange between the two superpowers, he contacted American intelligence and offered to pass secrets about the Soviet plans to the United States. He became a spy to save his country.

~~~~~~~~~~~~~~~~~~~~~~~~~~~~~~~~~~~~~~~~~~~~~~

## SPYING FOR A CAUSE—IDEOLOGY

Some spies work to support a cause or ideal they believe in or support. This might include gathering proof of human rights abuses in another country (as J. K. did) or spying on a foreign government in order to defeat its leaders and end the oppression of the citizens there.

The Death Eaters are one example of spying for a cause, even though they are not part of any government (at least not until they take over the Ministry of Magic). Lucius Malfoy spends a lot of time at the Ministry of Magic (Spying? Or as an agent of influence?), and upon the return of Voldemort Mr. Malfoy obtains information and relays it back to the Dark Lord. Death Eaters such as Lucius Malfoy are loyal not only to the Dark Lord but to what he believes: that pure-blooded wizards and witches (those with no Muggle ancestors) should have all the power and respect, and everyone else should be treated as inferior.

The Wizarding world provides several examples of spies who work for a personal cause (ideology). One is Draco Malfoy, who agrees to spy for Voldemort in order to get revenge after his father is exposed as a Death Eater and imprisoned in Azkaban. Draco is also an example of how unreliable a spy for a

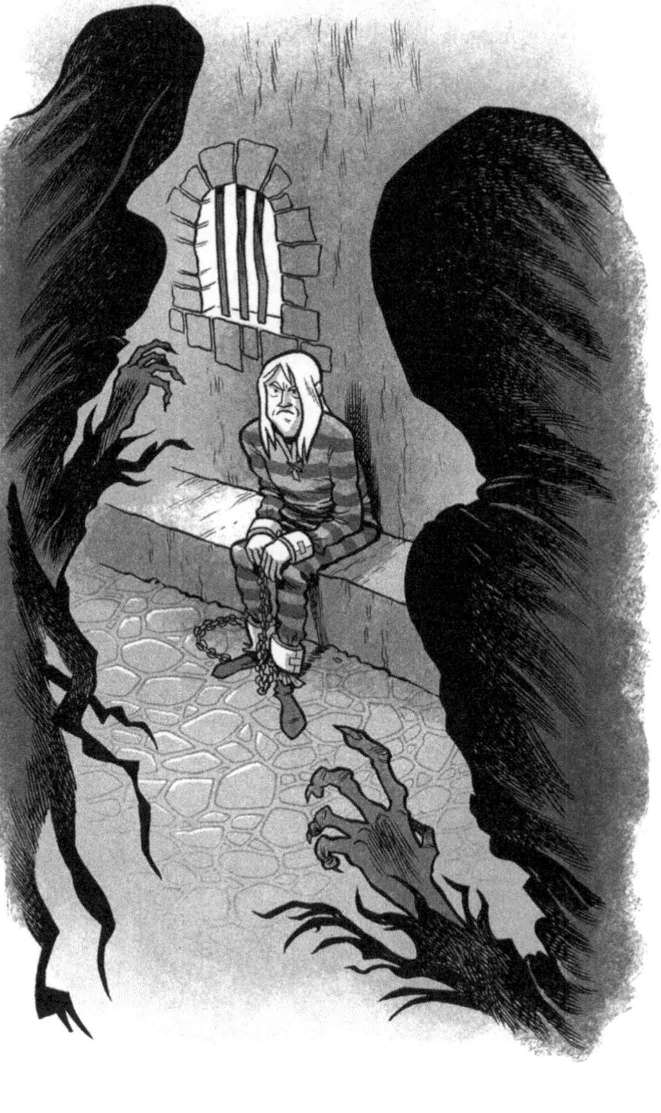

cause can be: when he realizes that Voldemort is using him, his loyalty wavers, but he continues to do his bidding because he knows Voldemort will kill him (and his parents) if he ceases to work for him.

Another example of someone spying for a cause is Professor Severus Snape, who switches his loyalty from Voldemort to Dumbledore, motivated by his love for Lily Evans—that is, Lily Potter, Harry's mother. Snape dedicates the rest of his life to protecting Harry and later spying on Voldemort, all to protect Lily's son. He is an excellent spy, right up to the sacrifice that proves his complete loyalty to Lily, and the boy he never liked.

## MADE TO SPY—COERCION

There are also persons who are forced to work for someone (and even spy for someone) due to **blackmail** or coercion. For example, in *Harry Potter and the Deathly Hallows*, Xenophilius Lovegood does Voldemort's bidding because his daughter, Luna, has been kidnapped by Death Eaters. And of course, in the Wizarding world we have unwilling "spies" or agents that have been placed under the Imperius Curse and do whatever they have been forced to do.

## LOVING TO SPY—EGO

People take up spying for other reasons as well. Some enjoy the adventure and excitement of the job: think of the Weasley twins, for example, or of James Bond, who is dedicated to

Her Majesty's Secret Service but loves the excitement as well. Wanting to know things that others do not know is based at least in part on ego. Getting back at a colleague or even your country can also be a form of ego—based on the desire to get even.

Whatever their motivation, spies are passionate about gathering information and getting it into the hands of those who can make the most use of it. In the next chapter, we'll talk about how spies work, from reading the daily paper to going deep undercover.

# CHAPTER 1

# ACTIVITIES

Help
**Nearly Headless Nick**
Navigate the moving staircases to the
**GRYFFINDOR**
Common Room!

## 1-2. BREAKING THE CODE – THE MIRROR OF ERISED

Remember the words on the top of the Mirror of Erised?

**Erised stra ehru oyt ube cafru oyt on wohsi.**

Can you break this code?
Here is a hint: *It is what was written on the top of the Mirror of Erised* (SS 207). A mirror!

When you look into a mirror, what do you see?
Second Hint: *Ignore the spacing.*

**ANSWER:** _____

_____

# 13. MATCHING – MATCH THE PATRONUS – PART 1

Draw a line from the person to his or her Patronus
(Remember, some persons have the same one!).

**Doe**

Harry Potter (*PA* 411)

**Otter**        James Potter (*PA* 424)        **Stag**

Hermione (*OP* 607)

Lily Potter (*DH* 687)

Severus Snape (*DH* 366)

**Phoenix**      Dumbledore (*DH* 390)      **Terrier**

Aberforth (*DH* 558, 560)

Ron (*DH* 648)

Ginny (Movie *OP* 1:22:15)

**Goat**                                         **Stallion**

## 1·4. MATCHING – SPY TERMS IN THE HARRY POTTER SERIES FOR FIRST YEARS

Match the word with the term by putting the number of the term in the blank.

**1. agent**          _____ Using information about someone to force them to do something for you. *Example:* By threatening to disclose Rita Skeeter as an unregistered Animagus, Hermione gets Rita to write a true article about what happened to Harry at the end of the Triwizard Tournament, when Voldemort returned.

**2. asset**          _____ An alternative name for a person or thing that is known only to a limited number of people. *Example:* When Harry writes to his godfather, Sirius, he refers to him as Snuffles.

**3. blackmail**          _____ Something of value; in the spy world, an individual, technology, or other means to obtain intelligence. *Example:* Each time Harry is moved from number four, Privet Drive, members of the Order of the Phoenix protect him.

**4. code name**          _____ An individual who is hired or employed by a country to spy. *Example:* Professor Quirrell served as one for Voldemort, assisting him in regaining his corporeal body.

# 1.5. MATCHING – SPY TERMS IN THE HARRY POTTER SERIES FOR SECOND YEARS

Match the word with the term by putting the number of the term in the blank.

**5. code breaking**

_____ A person who transfers a message from an agent to some other person or to headquarters. *Example:* Throughout the Harry Potter series, owls are used to send messages.

**6. concealment**

_____ The art of taking a message and extrapolating its content. *Example:* The inscription on the Mirror of Erised, "Erised stra ehru oyt ube cafru oyt on wohsi" (*SS* 207), is actually a single sentence in English.

**7. courier**

_____ A change of apparel or appearance that makes a person unrecognizable. *Example:* Barty Crouch Jr., through the use of Polyjuice Potion, appears to be Professor Alastor Moody.

**8. disguise**

_____ The act of hiding something, often in plain sight. *Example:* Harry's Invisibility Cloak assists him on numerous occasions in not being seen.

# 1·6. CHRONOLOGY – CHRONOLOGY OF HOGWARTS' DEFENSE AGAINST THE DARK ARTS TEACHERS

How well did you do at Hogwarts all seven years? Can you put the names of the Defense Against the Dark Arts teachers in order, from year 1 to year 7 ?

Here are the teachers: Amycus **Carrow**, Gilderoy **Lockhart**, Remus J. **Lupin**, Alastor "Mad-Eye" **Moody**, Professor **Quirrell**, Severus **Snape**, and Dolores **Umbridge**.

**Year 1.** _____
*Harry Potter and the Sorcerer's Stone*

**Year 2.** _____
*Harry Potter and the Chamber of Secrets*

**Year 3.** _____
*Harry Potter and the Prisoner of Azkaban*

**Year 4.** _____
*Harry Potter and the Goblet of Fire*

**Year 5.** _____
*Harry Potter and the Order of the Phoenix*

**Year 6.** _____
*Harry Potter and the Half-Blood Prince*

**Year 7.** _____
*Harry Potter and the Deathly Hallows*

# 1·7. WORD SEARCH – PETS AND THEIR OWNERS

Do your best to find all of the Harry Potter
pets and their owners.

```
P E R C Y E R O D E L B M U D
I H X N Y N E V I L L E S V W
G E N O I M R E H T Y R R A H
W D B R C R O O K S H A N K S
I W E L L D F A W K E S O M C
D I R G A H E P O T G Y R H A
G G R J O B Z F R O F I B I B
E A O U K U S E G F S S E E B
O Y L C Z X V A U N O T R T E
N R U S S O R L R P O T T E R
Z B T T R A F W E A S L E Y S
```

## *Find:*

❑ Trevor          ❑ Errol          ❑ Crookshanks     ❑ Hedwig
❑ Fluffy          ❑ Buckbeak       ❑ Aragog          ❑ Norbert
❑ Scabbers        ❑ Fawkes         ❑ Pigwidgeon      ❑ Hagrid
❑ Ron             ❑ Harry          ❑ Neville         ❑ Percy
❑ Potter          ❑ Weasleys       ❑ Hermione        ❑ Dumbledore

# 1·8. FILL IN THE BLANK – THE LIFE OF J. K. ROWLING (THE EARLY YEARS) – PART 1

How well do you know the Jo Rowling? Here is your chance to discover the details of her life and the sources of many of the Harry Potter characters. Just fill in the blank, if you can!

1.  Jo's grandfathers happen to be named _____ and _____. One grandmother was named Kathleen, and the other loved dogs more than people (she became the basis for Aunt Marge). *Hint: Think of the names of the drivers of the Knight Bus.*

    **1. Answers:** _____ **and** _____

2.  Peter Rowling and his future bride, Ann, met on a _____ in 1963 on his way from London to his military postings in Scotland. *Hint: Jo first envisioned the Harry Potter series while riding one of these.*

    **2. Answer:** _____

3.  Joanne _____ Rowling is born, _____ _____ , 1966. *Hint: Her middle name is from her grandmother, and her birthday happens to be the same as Harry Potter's birthday.*

    **3. Answers:** _____ **and** _____ _____

4.  At age four when Jo is sick with measles, her father reads her a well-known English classic _____, which provides Jo her most vivid early childhood memory. *Hint: It features a toad, a badger, and weasels.*

    **4. Answer:** _____ _____ _____ _____ _____ **(5 words)**

**5.** By age four Jo is making up stories for her younger sister, _____. *Hint: What is the name of England's Prince Harry's mother?*

   **5. Answer:** _____

**6.** By age six Jo writes her first story about a _____ and a giant bee, which she names Miss Bee. *Hint: Think of what is Luna's Patronus.*

   **6. Answer:** _____

**7.** Jo's very tiny dog was named _____. *Hint: Name the rabbit in Bambi.*

   **7. Answer:** _____

**8.** The Rowlings moved to a new town and Jo became friends with a brother and sister named Ian and Vikki _____, with whom they played Jo's favorite game: witches and wizards!

   **8. Answer:** _____

**9.** Jo at age nine moves to Tutshill, in the Forest of _____. *Hint: Think of where Harry, Ron, and Hermione hide in book 7.*

   **9. Answer:** _____

**10.** At Tutshill Jo lives in a cottage next to a church, which happens to have a _____that the kids regularly play in, without being scared at all! *Hint: Jo admits going to these to discover interesting names to use in her writings.*

   **10. Answer:** _____

## 1.9. FILL IN THE BLANK – THE LIFE OF SEVERUS SNAPE (THE EARLY YEARS) – PART 1

How well do you know Severus Snape, in chronological order of his life? Here is your chance to discover the details of his life and how he became the best double agent ever. Just fill in the blank, if you can!

1.  Snape, as a young child, cries in a corner while his father shouts at his cowering _____ (*OP* 591).

    **1. Answer:** _____

2.  Snape, with greasy hair, shoots _____ with his wand while sitting in his room (*OP* 591).

    **2. Answer:** _____

3.  Snape meets _____ and _____ Evans (*DH* 662–65).

    **3. Answers:** _____ **and** _____

4.  Snape tells Lily Evans about the _____ world (*DH* 665–67).

    **4. Answer:** _____

5.  Snape observes Lily at the train station talking to Petunia about her letter to _____ and the letter from Dumbledore to Petunia (*DH* 668–70).

    **5. Answer:** _____

**6.** Snape, on the Hogwarts Express with Lily Evans, meets
_____ _____ and _____ _____
(*DH* 670–72), two boys who immediately taunt Snape.

**6. Answers:** _____ _____ **and** _____

_____

**7.** Snape, Lily, James, and the others are sorted into
_____. (*DH* 672)

**7. Answer:** _____

**8.** A girl laughs at Snape as he tries to mount a bucking
_____ (*OP* 591).

**8. Answer:** _____

**9.** Snape suspects that _____ _____ is a werewolf:
Snape learns from _____ _____ how to get past
the _____ _____ and follows Lupin into the
tunnel; _____ _____ then rescues Snape and
saves his life (*SS* 300; *PA* 356–57; *DH* 673–74), something
Snape never forgives him for doing.

**9. Answers:** _____ _____

_____ _____

_____ _____

_____ _____

# CHAPTER 1

# ANSWERS

# FRONT FLAP. ANSWERS TO MAZE FRONT FLAP – HELP HARRY GRAB THE DRAGON'S EGG

## 1·1. ANSWERS TO MAZE – HELP NEARLY·HEADLESS NICK FIND THE GRYFFINDOR COMMON ROOM

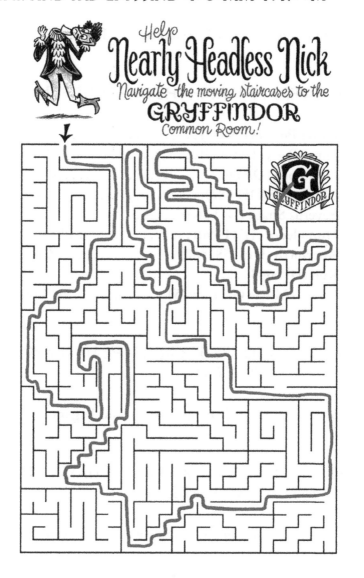

## 1·2. ANSWERS TO BREAKING THE CODE 1 – THE MIRROR OF ERISED:

I show not your face but your heart's desire.

## 1·3. ANSWERS TO MATCH THE PATRONUS – PART 1:

Harry Potter (PA 411) . . . . . . . . . . . . . . . . . . . .Stag
James Potter (PA 424) . . . . . . . . . . . . . . . . . . . .Stag
Hermione (OP 607). . . . . . . . . . . . . . . . . . . . .Otter
Lily Potter (DH 687). . . . . . . . . . . . . . . . . . . . .Doe
Severus Snape (DH 366) . . . . . . . . . . . . . . . . .Doe
Dumbledore (DH 390) . . . . . . . . . . . . . . . . Phoenix
Aberforth (DH 558, 560) . . . . . . . . . . . . . . . . Goat
Ron (DH 648) . . . . . . . . . . . . . . . . . . . . . . . Terrier
Ginny (Movie OP 1:22:15) . . . . . . . . . . . . Stallion

## 1·4. ANSWERS TO SPY TERMS IN THE HARRY POTTER SERIES FOR FIRST YEARS:

3 blackmail, 4 code name, 2 asset, and 1 agent

## 1·5. ANSWERS TO SPY TERMS IN THE HARRY POTTER SERIES FOR SECOND YEARS:

7 courier, 5 code breaking, 8 disguise, and 6 concealment

# 1·6. ANSWERS TO CHRONOLOGY OF HOGWARTS DEFENSE AGAINST THE DARK ARTS TEACHERS:

1. **Professor Quirrell**
2. **Gilderoy Lockhart**
3. **Remus J. Lupin**
4. **Alastor "Mad-Eye" Moody**
5. **Dolores Umbridge**
6. **Severus Snape**
7. **Amycus Carrow**

# 1·7. ANSWERS TO WORD SEARCH – PETS AND THEIR OWNERS:

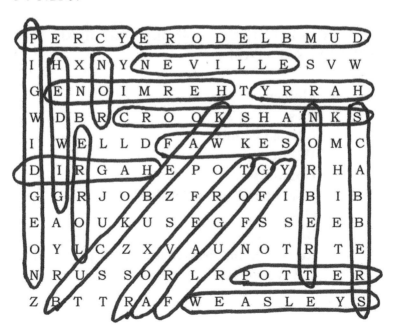

## 1·8. ANSWERS TO FILL IN THE BLANK – THE LIFE OF J. K. ROWLING (EARLY YEARS) – PART 1:

1. Ernie and Stanley
2. train
3. Kathleen and July 31
4. *The Wind in the Willows*
5. Di
6. rabbit
7. Thumper
8. Potter
9. Dean
10. graveyard

## 1·9. ANSWERS TO THE LIFE OF SEVERUS SNAPE (THE EARLY YEARS) – PART 1

1. Mother
2. flies
3. Lily and Petunia
4. Wizarding
5. Hogwarts
6. James Potter and Sirius Black
7. Houses
8. Broomstick
9. Remus Lupin, Sirius Black, Whomping Willow, and James Potter

# Chapter 2
## LEARNING SECRETS: HOW SPIES WORK

Just as there are different kinds of spies, there are also different kinds of spy work. A case officer who attends a government official's party with the intent of stealing information has a very different job than an agent who has agreed to secretly pass information to a case officer. And back at **headquarters**, analysts spend substantial time organizing information gathered by case officers stationed throughout the world—along with other information—analyzing it for use by government policy-makers.

## CASE OFFICERS

Case officers are what most people think of when they imagine spying: people who gather information relating to all countries and organizations throughout the world, especially those that are adversarial to us. Case officers spend most of their time trying to recruit agents to spy for them. To be good at this, case officers have to have a low profile. One of the most essential aspects of spying is the ability to blend in. That's because the most effective spy is someone who doesn't look like a spy at all!

## COVER STORIES

When a case officer takes a spying assignment, it usually includes a **cover story** that explains the case officer's presence in the area where she or he is gathering information. It is common for case officers to be assigned to seemingly boring jobs with some U.S. government affiliation.

Maintaining cover is very important to a spy's work. If a person has a good reason for being in a certain place at a certain time, others will be less suspicious of that person. So it is important for a spy to spend a lot of time making his or her cover look real. If a spy's cover story is that he or she works a desk job, that spy must show up for work regularly like everybody else in the office and do at least some of the work.

Kingsley Shacklebolt, who spies on the Ministry of Magic for the Order of the Phoenix, has the perfect cover by already being in the right position. He is already working for the Ministry as an Auror when Voldemort returns (rather spectacularly) during Harry's first year at Hogwarts. Later, when the Ministry chooses to deny that the Dark Lord has returned and blames Sirius Black for Voldemort's crimes, Shacklebolt is assigned the task of tracking down Sirius—thus giving the Order of the Phoenix **access** to all of the information it needs to keep Sirius safe. But Shacklebolt can't just stop turning up for work when the Order has a problem, nor can he argue with his bosses about Sirius's innocence. In order to maintain his cover, he has to act like a loyal Ministry employee—pretending to search for Sirius while in reality protecting him!

## SPY TERMS: ACCESS

In the intelligence world, having **access** means that you are privy to information that is limited to a select number of people. For example, in the world of Harry Potter only a few people have access to the location of the headquarters of the Order of the Phoenix at number twelve, Grimmauld Place.

---

Not all cover stories, or *legends,* are easily made up. As Dumbledore's spy, Mrs. Figg is assigned a cover story as a nice, little old lady who happens to live (with all her cats) near the Dursleys . . . and incidentally their orphaned nephew, Harry Potter. If Dumbledore sent wizards and witches (as opposed to a Squib) to follow Harry during the summer months and watch his every move, everyone in the neighborhood would know that something wasn't right. (The Ministry would also know because they keep track of any wizards or witches who reside near the Dursley's home.) But nobody thinks twice when a nosy neighbor keeps an eye on the kids next door—the Dursleys even ask Mrs. Figg to babysit Harry when they don't want him around. How convenient! They never even suspect that she is an undercover spy for Dumbledore. She lived her legend for *fifteen years* before she breaks cover the night that Harry and Dudley are attacked by Dementors in Little Whinging, telling Harry, "Don't put it away, idiot boy! What if there are more of them around?"

---

## SPY TERMS: COVER STORIES

A cover story, or legend, is a detailed false history of a person. The best cover stories stick close to the truth: if you've lived all your life in the United States, for instance, it will be hard to convince someone that

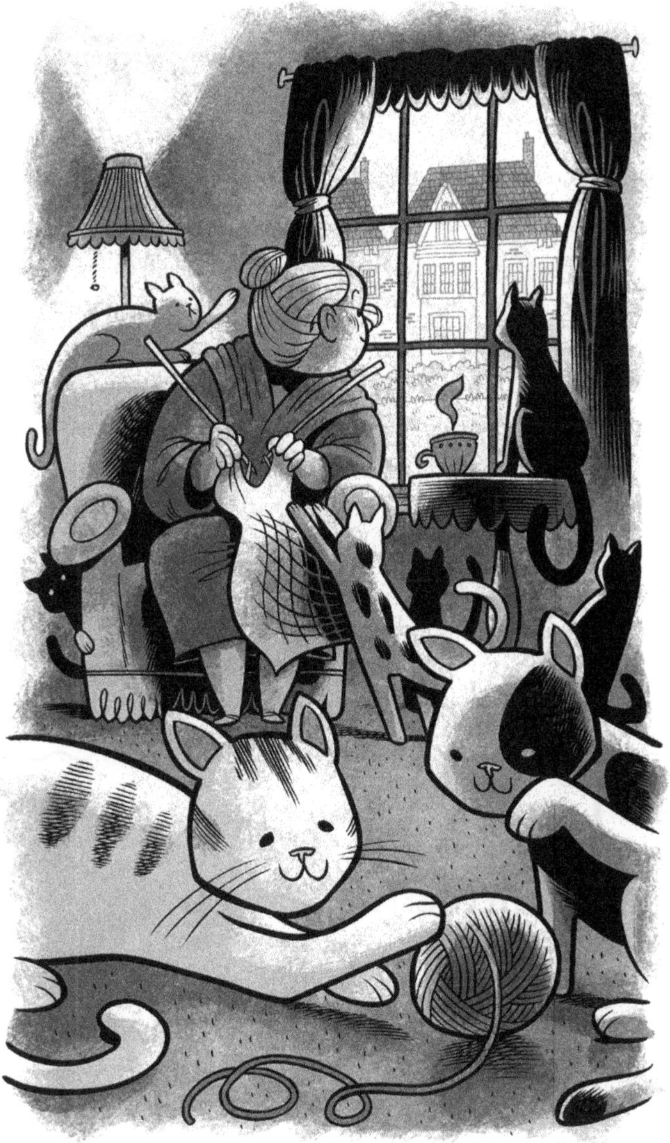

you grew up in Poland! Cover stories often involve the creation of fake records that provide backup for the story, such as fake identification, a résumé with an invented job history, and even bank accounts under an assumed name.

Spies aren't the only ones who create cover stories. The Dursleys created several cover stories to explain Harry's presence in their home and, later, his disappearance during the school year. In *Harry Potter and the Sorcerer's Stone,* we learn that they told Harry that his parents had died in a car crash. Later, in *Harry Potter and the Prisoner of Azkaban,* the Dursleys admit to creating another cover story to explain why Harry is gone during the school year, claiming that he attends school at St. Brutus's Secure Center for Incurably Criminal Boys. Thus, even those not in the intelligence world create cover stories to hide things.

## DEFINING INTELLIGENCE

**Intelligence** in the spy world usually refers to information not readily available. Intelligence can be information that is secret and is in the hands of a small number of people who have access to that information, as well as information that is out in the public.

Examples of restricted information include everything

from the secret recipe for Coca-Cola to the travel arrangements for the president of the United States. Case officers go undercover in order to get access to **inside information**. Once a case officer has established a solid presence in his or her cover, he or she might use the cover position to acquire secret information, as well as public information or **open source intelligence**. That might involve scheduling a meeting with an official of the foreign government in order to plant a listening device in the official's office, or finagling an invitation to a party at the home of an important business person in order to sneak into that person's office and hunt for documents. Even getting the chance to walk through a building can generate inside information, such as the case officer getting the opportunity to observe the layout and location of important offices or back entrances in an unfamiliar place.

In *Harry Potter and the Order of the Phoenix*, Harry finds out in one of his visions that Voldemort is getting inside intelligence about the Department of Mysteries from the escaped Death Eater Augustus Rookwood, who once worked there. Thanks to his mysterious connection to Voldemort, Harry "sees" this inside information provided by none other than Voldemort himself. Through this vision Harry finds out that Lucius Malfoy has used the Imperius Curse to force another Ministry employee, Broderick Bode, to spy for him. Muggle spies can't read the minds of their adversaries, but they may be able to "see" what is going on by using spies and technology.

Open source intelligence is information available to everyone. It includes public media such as television broadcasts and newspaper articles, websites and social media, reports and speeches by government officials, and anything else that is free for the taking. Harry, Hermione, and Ron regularly read the *Daily Prophet* in search of open source intelligence. As you may remember from the books, however, such intelligence isn't always accurate. Like any other **source** of free information, the *Daily Prophet*'s articles are sometimes incorrect, incomplete, or **biased**—that is, they twist information in order to benefit some people at the expense of others. Experienced spies gather up as much open source intelligence as possible and then sift through it, comparing what they have observed and know about their subject to what they find in these sources, all in order to figure out the truth.

In the final book, *Harry Potter and the Deathly Hallows*, our three friends—in their attempt to get into Umbridge's office and retrieve the locket—observe the comings and goings of Ministry employees to figure out a way to get into the Ministry of Magic covertly. This is technically open source information.

The intelligence community subdivides intelligence into various groupings. For example, HUMINT, or *human intelligence,* is any information obtained directly from people, whether that person offers to share what they saw and heard during a vacation in a foreign country or passes information obtained secretly from an opponent's headquarters. SIGINT, or *signals intelligence*, is information obtained from the various methods of intercepting signals, such as radar and sonar, as well as intercepted communications from telephone and Internet systems.

# INTELLIGENCE ANALYSTS

Information collected by case officers is subsequently reviewed by analysts. These "desk spies" or intelligence analysts use computers and their own careful study of intelligence gathered by case officers as well as other sources of intelligence, such as information acquired from cell-phone communications and Internet records.

Intelligence analysts do not face the same time pressures as a spy cracking a safe, but they are under pressure to evaluate the massive amounts of intelligence and come up with conclusions promptly. Analysts must always keep an open mind about the information they're analyzing. In fact, the intelligence community (the sixteen intelligence agencies in the United States and the Director of National Intelligence) depends on the willingness of its analysts to question *everything* in order to avoid making poor assumptions or basing decisions on weak or incorrect information.

In *Harry Potter and the Deathly Hallows*, Harry, Ron, and Hermione serve as intelligence analysts to locate the Horcruxes. They realize that each item used by Voldemort as a Horcrux will be significant and probably relates to each of the Hogwarts' houses. Indeed, Tom Riddle's first job was obtaining wizarding artifacts for Borgin and Burkes. By superb analysis and taking into account the information about the previously discovered Horcruxes (a certain diary and ring that Dumbledore had located and rashly placed on his finger), our three friends are able to locate a locket, a cup, and a diadem, and figure out how to destroy them. When Harry and his friends put together all of the information they have gathered, they are able to look for patterns and unusual occurrences that add up to something more than the individual data points. It takes persistence and patience to sort through all of the information you have and decide what information is important, especially when the most important information can look like it is not important at all!

## MANY KINDS OF INTELLIGENCE OFFICERS

There are many different jobs available in the intelligence world, beyond just spying and intelligence **analysis**. For example, in the United States, the Central Intelligence Agency (CIA) needs research scientists, lawyers and paralegals, foreign language teachers, engineers, telecommunications and information technology specialists, accountants, editors and graphic designers, librarians for their in-house resources, and building maintenance crews. Each of these positions requires a detailed **background check** and special training for working in high-security buildings with access to sensitive information.

Peter Earnest spent more than twenty-five years in the CIA's clandestine service—that is, doing the kind of work that many people think of as spying. However, Peter also served as an inspector with the Office of Inspector General for the CIA, making sure that the agency worked efficiently and within the bounds of law. Later, he became the CIA's director of media relations, sharing information about the agency with the public and even arranging for the filming of part of the 1992 film *Patriot Games*, starring Harrison Ford, at the CIA's headquarters in Langley, VA. (Peter was even invited to appear as an extra in one of the scenes, but unfortunately, that footage ended up on the cutting-room floor.)

## SENIOR INTELLIGENCE OFFICERS: THE HANDLERS

The CIA is run by the director of the CIA. Within the agency is the Clandestine Service, which has case officers who get stationed all over the world. They gather intelligence and recruit others to spy for them. They receive their orders from their managers, who are usually senior case officers who relay the specific information needed or the target (person, entity, or even government).

In Harry Potter's world, Mad-Eye Moody often acts as a senior case officer, coordinating the efforts of the Order of the Phoenix and organizing missions, such as rescuing Harry from number four, Privet Drive. The overall director of the activities of the Order of the Phoenix is, of course, Albus Dumbledore himself. On the other side, Voldemort directs his own spy teams, including the undercover agents in the Ministry of Magic and Draco Malfoy, who at one point is assigned to kill Dumbledore.

## THE ROLE OF CASE OFFICERS

A case officer gathers information and recruits members of the opposing government or organization in order to create agents on the opposing side.

---

## CASE OFFICER/AGENT

Remember, a *case officer* is a member of your own intelligence organization, and an *agent* is a person who is recruited or volunteers to work for your organization.

~~~~~~~~~~~~~~~~~~~~~~

**Agents** are people who have been recruited by a case officer to provide information. Agents share information with the other side, often because they are unhappy with the current state of affairs, or because they see a chance for profit. A person may be targeted by the case officer for recruitment, or the individual may contact the case officer directly. The simplest way that a case officer gains agents is if the person wants to become a spy and is a **walk-in**. A walk-in is a person who volunteers to work for an intelligence service, sometimes by simply walking into the adversary's embassy or other location and offering to provide intelligence. Such agents often wish to see a change in how their country or organization works, but feel that they do not have enough power to make change themselves.

Agents who are bribed, however, will share information only when paid money (or sometimes given power or influence) in return for their information. Such agents can be useful, but there is always the possibility that an agent could become the adversary's agent if your adversary offers a better deal.

~~~~~~~~~~~~~~~~~~~~~~

## BUMBLERS AND KLUTZES: NOT WHAT THEY SEEM

The best spies are smart, talented people—but sometimes they don't seem that way! Being a bumbler or a klutz can be both a disguise and a work of art. Think of Clark Kent, Superman's dorky alter ego. You never know whether a bumbler is the dumbest person you have ever met, or the most brilliant. Think back to Professor Quirrell in *Harry Potter and the Sorcerer's Stone*—as Quirrell himself says when he finally confronts Harry, "Who would suspect p-p-poor, st-stuttering P-Professor Quirrell?" (*SS* 288). He looks helpless, even pathetic, but Voldemort is "running" Quirrell, using him as a mole: a long-term undercover spy. You never know whether a bumbler is harmless or powerful, or where his or her loyalties lie. In other words, judge people carefully, and don't make assumptions based on appearances alone.

## DOUBLE AGENTS

Double agents can be willing or unwilling recruits. Willing double agents are often unhappy with the situation in their own country or organization and want to help the opposing side instead. It is important to note that to be a double agent you have to first be working as a spy for Country A (*Always* the good guys), and then while being a spy for Country A you are "turned" and agree to work for Country B (*Bad* guys) *against* Country A. Country A still thinks you are loyal and working for them! So in the spy world, Snape is definitely a double agent because he joined the Death Eaters and was spying on Dumbledore, and then Dumbledore turned him back against Voldemort, all the while with Voldemort thinking that Snape was still loyal to him.

Unwilling double agents are those who have been forced, often through threats or blackmail, to spy on and against their original employers. And, of course, unscrupulous magic-users always have the option of using the Imperius Curse to make others spy involuntarily for them as well.

When an agent agrees to work for the other side, the person is said to have been "turned" by the organization or person that convinced him or her to switch sides. The best example of this in the world of Harry Potter is Severus Snape, who was turned from Voldemort's side by Professor Dumbledore himself after Snape learned that the Dark Lord planned to kill Lily Potter (and her family). Snape becomes one of the most talented double agents ever, hiding his allegiance not only from Lord Voldemort—at a terrible risk—but even from many of those he intends to help, especially Harry.

## MOLES AND SLEEPER AGENTS: THE LONG GAME

Some of the hardest spy jobs are the long-term missions, perhaps years in the making and years in the waiting.

**Moles** are persons who work for Organization B (*Bad* guys) and agree to provide information to Organization A (*Always* the good guys). The mole may have been previously working for Organization B, or that person may have joined Organization B at the direction of Organization A. Moles are in a position to receive and gather important information. Persons who have been trusted members of Organization B for a long time are often safe from discovery and less likely to fall under suspicion. They go about their usual business, quietly providing intelligence to the case officer of Organization A. Once a mole has been placed in an organization or government, patience is the key. A mole must often land a job at the target organization and actually work there, as a "loyal" employee, for many years before getting access to key information. That agent must often stick to his or her cover story for years in order to gain the trust of other people in the organization.

An example from Harry's story is Professor Quirrell, who spends an entire year teaching at Hogwarts while secretly serving Voldemort's quest to return to a human body. Kingsley Shacklebolt works as a mole in *Harry Potter and the Order of the Phoenix*, thanks to his position as an Auror. The Ministry of Magic is confident that Shacklebolt is a loyal employee, and thus he gets sensitive assignments, such as tracking the whereabouts of Sirius Black and accompanying Cornelius Fudge when Professor Umbridge exposes the activities of Dumbledore's Army. But he is a mole. Shacklebolt is actually loyal to the Order of the Phoenix, and he is a valuable source—for the Order of the Phoenix—of inside intelligence about the Ministry.

To maintain his cover story, Shacklebolt cannot act directly to help Harry when the Ministry tries to get him expelled—he must hide his loyalties, even to the point of being knocked out along with the rest of the Ministry's employees as Dumbledore escapes arrest. When Kingsley is assigned to "assist" the British Muggle Prime Minister on behalf of the Ministry of Magic, he is actually serving as a mole, but this time for the Ministry of Magic.

Spies like Mrs. Figg are known as **sleeper agents**. They live deep undercover for a long period of time until an order or event causes them to spring into action. When Harry leaves the safety of number four, Privet Drive in *Harry Potter and the Order of the Phoenix*, Mrs. Figg apparently goes searching for Harry—and finds him just as he is using his Patronus to save himself and Cousin Dudley. Sleeper agents may lie in wait and not communicate with headquarters at all, or may be required occasionally to report items of interest, depending on their specific assignment. They may or may not be assigned to provide information during that time.

It takes a lot of work to set up a successful long-term undercover spy. The longer the agent can maintain cover, the deeper the cover. Long-term spies may start families, build homes, own businesses, and even vote like regular citizens. In 2010, eleven people were arrested in the United States on suspicion of being deep-cover spies for the Russian government.

One couple, known as Richard and Cynthia Murphy, lived in a New Jersey suburb with their two daughters; he worked as an architect, and she worked in finance. However, agents of the **Federal Bureau of Investigation (FBI)** had been tracking them for years and stated that the pair had been using their business and social connections to collect open source information about the U.S. political and economic decisions for spymasters in Moscow. Once found, they were deported to Russia—probably to the great shock of their teenage kids, who had assumed they were Americans.

## SNEAKING INTO DENIED AREAS

A *denied area* is a country where it is very difficult for an intelligence officer to go. During the Cold War, it included the Soviet Union and the countries allied with the Soviet Union. In today's world, this would include countries where we have an official presence, such as having embassies, but where it is still very difficult to operate, such as China. North Korea would certainly be considered a denied area.

While writing his spy novel *Mission to Chara*, Lynn wanted to make it as accurate as possible. To do that, he traveled to Chara, a small town in Siberia, about three hundred miles north of the northernmost portion of China, shortly after the fall of the Soviet Union. Because Chara was close to a Russian military base and was a denied area for foreign travelers, Lynn obtained a visa to visit a popular Russian tourist city about three hundred miles west of Chara and another approved city about four hundred miles east of Chara.

Flying Aeroflot from Moscow to Omsk and then Bratsk, Lynn planned on traveling across Siberia on the Baikal–Amur Mainline railroad, which passed through Chara. However, Lynn was not able to purchase a ticket on the train because the only person who could sell foreigner tickets was gone for the next three or four days.

So, like any resourceful intelligence officer, Lynn's translator convinced a local person to allow Lynn to purchase the ticket to Chara using that person's passport, thus requiring Lynn to assume that person's identity for the rest of the three-day train ride to Chara—and back.

~~~~~~~~~~~~~~~~~~~~~~~~~~~~~~~~~~~~~~

## GETTING THE JOB DONE

Let's review how different kinds of spies get their jobs done.

In a sense, the essence of spying is listening in on people who do not know that you are listening. The word *eavesdropping* comes from the historical spying practice of hanging from somebody's eaves—the edge of the roof—and listening at their window, an old English tradition. With the development of

electronics, the term now relates to much more sophisticated means, such as hidden microphones (or **"bugs"**), laser microphones that can "hear" conversations inside the building through the vibrations of the windowpanes, and good old-fashioned wiretapping, whether on the wires of landline phones or, more recently, the interception of electronic cell phone signals. In *Harry Potter and the Goblet of Fire*, Rita Skeeter actually listens in as a real bug to gather information!

Once the spy is assigned a mission to target a person or

organization, the first thing the case officer needs, of course, is the available information about the target. The information might tell the case officer where in a building to go, when security guards or employees are likely to be around, and what information or documents need to be obtained.

Spies frequently set out to acquire copies of critical information. They might photograph or make copies of **classified** documents, make maps of targeted territories or buildings with the locations of information caches, capture video footage of the adversary's agents or employees in action, copy digital documents onto memory sticks, or steal original documents. Stealing is a last resort in many cases, however. Remember, the best spy is the one you never know was there. If documents have disappeared from a safe, the other side can be certain that something has gone wrong! It's much better to make copies or photographs and then leave everything exactly as the spy found it, with no trace of anyone who wasn't supposed to be there.

## THE COVERT PLUMBING SERVICE

During Peter's service in the CIA, he joined several tech officers on an operation to break into the home of a Soviet intelligence officer and bug the house while the man was away for the weekend. After planting listening devices on the main floor, they went down to the basement to finish. A few moments later, however, one of the officers realized that the basement was slowly filling with water. Somehow, they had broken a water pipe and sprung a leak! It took all evening and into the early morning hours to repair the damage and leave the basement looking exactly as they had found it. The vacationing intelligence officer never knew that he'd gotten some extremely expensive plumbing assistance from his U.S. counterparts!

The Weasley twins developed a supurb listening device, Extendable Ears, and found out substantial information by using this wonderful invention—that is, until Mrs. Weasley applied a counterjinx!

# DELIVERING THE GOODS

Once the spy has collected the targeted information, he or she must get that information back to the organization without being discovered. The case officer working undercover must deliver information without raising suspicions regarding the cover story. The information might be left at a previously selected place (dead drop), or it might be sent over the Internet in an untraceable, encoded file.

## SPY TERMS: HEADQUARTERS

Headquarters is the place from which an intelligence organization is based. For example, the headquarters of the Order of the Phoenix is at number twelve, Grimmauld Place.

In the next chapter, we'll talk about spy communications and how case officers can communicate without being intercepted.

# CHAPTER 2

# ACTIVITIES

# 2·1. MAZE

Help the **Fat Friar** find the HUFFLEPUFF Common Room!

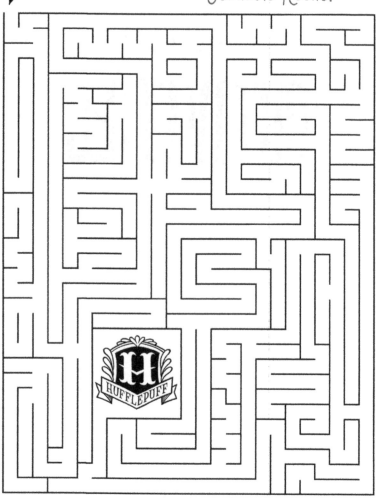

## 2.2. BREAKING THE CODE – 6 – 2 – 4 – 4 – 2

Remember Harry in book 5, *Order of the Phoenix*, when he has to go to the Ministry of Magic for his trial for using magic to defend himself and Cousin Dudley against the dementors?

Harry enters through the visitor's entrance to the Ministry of Magic—a phone booth—and Mr. Weasley dials "six . . . two . . . four . . . and another four . . . and another two." (125)

*Do you know what the numbers 6 – 2 – 4 – 4 – 2 mean?*

*It translates into one English word.*

Here's a hint: he is using a phone.
Here's another hint: phones list letters below each number.

6 M N O

2 A B C

4 G H I

4 G H I

2 A B C

Can you now decode 6 – 2 – 4 – 4 – 2?

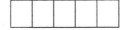

# 2·3. MATCHING – MATCH THE PATRONUS – PART 2

Draw a line from the person to his or her Patronus.

**Cat** (with markings around her eyes)

Cho (*OP* 606)

**Hare**　　　　　Mr. Weasley (*DH* 121)　　　　　**Boar**

Kingsley Shacklebolt (*DH* 159)

Umbridge (*DH* 259)

McGonagall (*DH* 596)

**Weasel**　　　　Luna (*DH* 649)　　　　**Lynx**

Ernie (*DH* 649)

Seamus (*DH* 649)

**Long-Haired Cat**　　　**Swan**　　　**Fox**

# 2.4. MATCHING - SPY TERMS IN THE HARRY POTTER SERIES FOR THIRD YEARS

Match the word with the term by putting the number of the term in the blank.

**9. diversion**  _____ An agent employed by one entity but working in reality for another entity or person. *Example:* Snape is working for Dumbledore while at the same time spying on Voldemort, who thinks Snape is *his* agent!

**10. double agent**  _____ An occurrence that results in a person shifting attention away from the immediate situation or going elsewhere. *Example:* In order to assist Harry in getting into Professor Umbridge's office the first time, the Weasley twins use fireworks to get Umbridge away from her office.

**11. eavesdropping**  _____ A person assigned to warn others if someone approaches during a covert operation. *Example:* Ginny and Luna serve as these when Harry sneaks into Professor Umbridge's office the second time.

**12. lookout**  _____ Surreptitiously listening to someone's conversation. *Example:* As a young Death Eater, Snape listened in on Dumbledore as he met with Sybill Trelawney and overheard the first part of the prophecy, which he reported to Voldemort.

# 2.5. MATCHING – SPY TERMS IN THE HARRY POTTER SERIES FOR FOURTH YEARS

Match the word with the term by putting the number of the term in the blank.

**13. password**

_____ Any subtle action conveying a covert message or indication to take a preplanned action. *Example:* When Harry is being taken from Privet Drive by his security team in book 5, someone has been assigned to send up sparks into the air to indicate that it is safe to proceed.

**14. recruitment**

_____ A place where agents or defectors can be safely hidden; often a place to debrief agents. *Example:* Number twelve, Grimmauld Place, is used as one of these by the Order of the Phoenix throughout the last half of the series—until it is compromised.

**15. safe house**

_____ The act of getting someone to join your side. *Example:* Professor Dumbledore gets Slughorn to teach at Hogwarts at the beginning of book 6.

**16. signal**

_____ A word or number sequence that allows access to a building or information. *Example:* In order to get into Dumbledore's office, both the students and the teachers must use such a word.

# 2·6. CHRONOLOGY – CHRONOLOGY OF THE MINISTERS OF MAGIC

Can you put the names of the Ministers of Magic in order for the entire Harry Potter series?

Cornelius **Fudge**

Rufus **Scrimgeour**

Kingsley **Shacklebolt**

Pius **Thicknesse**

**Years 1–5.**                    1. _____
*Harry Potter and the Sorcerer's Stone*
*Harry Potter and the Chamber of Secrets*
*Harry Potter and the Prisoner of Azkaban*
*Harry Potter and the Goblet of Fire*
*Harry Potter and the Order of the Phoenix*

**Year 6–7.**                    2. _____
*Harry Potter and the Half-Blood Prince*
*Harry Potter and the Deathly Hollows*

**Year 7.**                    3. _____
*Harry Potter and the Deathly Hollows*

**End of Year 7 (temporary).**  4. _____
*Harry Potter and the Deathly Hollows*

# 2-7. FILL IN THE BLANK – THE LIFE OF J. K. ROWLING (THE SCHOOL YEARS) – PART 2

How well do you know Jo? Here is your chance to discover the details of her life and the sources of many of the Harry Potter characters. Just fill in the blank, if you can!

11. Around age nine, Jo discovers the _____ _____ series of spy novels written by Ian Fleming, first reading *Thunderball*, as well as the works of _____ _____, her favorite writer ever. *Hint: First half, 007; second half, this person wrote* Pride and Prejudice.

    11. Answer: _____ _____ and _____ _____

12. At her first day at Tutshill school, Jo's new teacher, Mrs. Morgan—who later becomes one of the sources for Professor _____—puts Jo in the "dim" row after she fails a test in _____. *Hint: numerator and denominator.*

    12. Answers: _____ and _____

13. Jo later attends Wyedean Comprehensive School and reads feminist author _____ Mitford's *Hons and Rebels* ("It changed my life"). *Hint: She names her daughter after this author.*

    13. Answer: _____

14. In her eleventh year in school, Jo sees her very first play, _____ _____ by William Shakespeare. *Hint: The king in this play has three daughters.*

    14. Answer: _____ _____

**15.** While still in high school, Jo also sees another Shakespeare play, *The Winter's Tale*, which has a female character named _____!

**15. Answer:** _____

**16.** Sean Harris moves to high school during Jo's last year and brings with him Jo's vehicle for freedom, a turquoise _____ _____. *Hint: Jo uses this as the Weasley's flying car (CS 66, 70, 79).*

**16. Answer:** _____ _____

**17.** In Jo's final year she is selected as _____ _____, then graduates (with high honors). *Hint: Harry's mum held this position when she attended Hogwarts, with James as the male counterpart (SS 55).*

**17. Answer:** _____ _____

**18.** Jo next attends Exeter University, studying _____.

**18. Answer:** _____

**19.** Jo spends one school year during college studying abroad in the European city of _____ as an assistant teacher.

**19. Answer:** _____

**20.** Jo graduates from Exeter University (with _____).

**20. Answer:** _____

## 2·8. FILL IN THE BLANK – THE LIFE OF SEVERUS SNAPE (THE VOLDEMORT YEARS) – PART 2

**10.** Lily objects to Snape's choice of friends, while Snape objects to the behavior of _____ _____ and his friends (*DH* 672–74).

**10. Answer:** _____ _____

**11.** Snape completes his O.W.L. in Defense Against the Dark Arts and wanders down by the lake, where he is bullied and taunted by _____ _____ but saved by _____ _____; Snape then calls the person who saved him a Mudblood (*OP* 640–48, *DH* 674).

**11. Answers:**

**Answers:** _____ _____ **and** _____ _____

**12.** Snape tries to apologize to _____ _____, who objects to Snape's Death Eater friends and claims he can't wait to join _____ (*DH* 675–76).

**12. Answers:**

_____ _____ **and** _____

**13.** Snape, now one of Voldemort's Death Eaters, serves as a messenger for Voldemort, delivering messages to _____ (*DH* 676).

**13. Answer:** _____

**14.** Snape overhears the first part of the _____, stating that the boy who can defeat the Dark Lord was born near the end of the month of _____ to parents who had thrice defeated _____ _____ _____ (three words) (*OP* 843; *DH* 677).

**14. Answers:**

_____ **and**

_____ **and**

_____ _____ _____ .

**15.** Snape then relays what he heard to _____ (*OP* 843; *DH* 677).

**15. Answer:** _____

# CHAPTER 2
# ANSWERS

## 2·1. ANSWER TO MAZE – HELP THE FAT FRIAR FIND THE HUFFLEPUFF COMMON ROOM

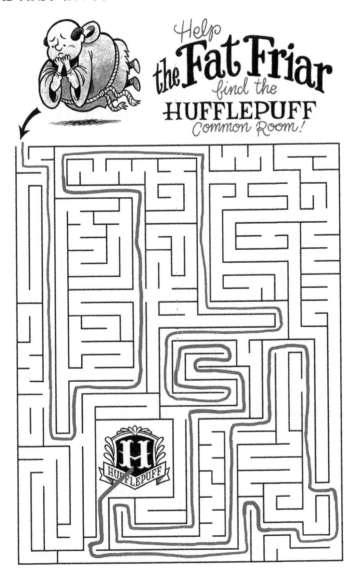

Help the **Fat Friar** find the **HUFFLEPUFF** Common Room!

## 2.2. ANSWER TO BREAKING THE CODE 2 – 6 – 2 – 4 – 4 – 2:

MAGIC!

## 2.3. ANSWERS TO MATCH THE PATRONESS (7TH YR):

Cho (OP 606) ............................ Swan
Mr. Weasley (DH 121) ................... Weasel
Kingsley Shacklebolt (DH 159)............... Lynx
Umbridge (DH 259) ............. Long-Haired Cat
McGonagall (DH 596) ....................... Cat
Luna (DH 649)............................ Hare
Ernie (DH 649) ........................... Boar
Seamus (DH 649)......................... Fox

## 2.4. ANSWERS TO SPY TERMS IN THE HARRY POTTER SERIES FOR THIRD YEARS:

10 double agent, 9 diversion, 12 lookout, and 11 eavesdropping

## 2.5. ANSWERS TO SPY TERMS IN THE HARRY POTTER SERIES FOR FOURTH YEARS:

16 signal, 15 safe house, 14 recruitment, and 13 password

## 2·6. ANSWERS TO CHRONOLOGY OF THE MINISTERS OF MAGIC:

Cornelius **Fudge**
Rufus **Scrimgeour**
Pius **Thicknesse**
Kingsley **Shacklebolt**

## 2·7. ANSWERS TO FILL IN THE BLANK – THE LIFE OF J. K. ROWLING (SCHOOL YEARS) – PART 2

11. **James Bond and Jane Austen**
12. **Snape and fractions**
13. **Jessica**
14. *King Lear*
15. **Hermione**
16. **Ford Anglia**
17. **Head Girl**
18. **French**
19. **Paris**
20. **honors**

# 2·8. ANSWERS TO THE LIFE OF SEVERUS SNAPE (THE VOLDEMORT YEARS) – PART 2

**10. James Potter**
**11. James Potter and Lily Evans**
**12. Lily Evans and Voldemort**
**13. Dumbledore**
**14. prophecy, July, and the Dark Lord**
**15. Voldemort**

# Chapter 3

## KEEPING SECRETS

In a field obsessed with keeping secrets, one of a spy's biggest concerns is communication. **Secure communication** is a two-way street: the person sending the information must send it in a way that it can't be intercepted, and the person or entity receiving the information must be able to keep it secure. Intelligence professionals spend a lot of time working to keep information secure.

## COMMUNICATION SECURITY

In the first chapters of *Harry Potter and the Order of the Phoenix*, Harry has a problem: his usual ways of communicating with his friends aren't working. In previous summers, owls brought frequent letters from Ron and Hermione, bearing all sorts of news about the Wizarding world. Harry relied on the owl post for friendly chatter as well as news of potential threats from his enemies. But this summer, his friends' letters have been brief and boring, with apologies like "can't say much" and "can't give you any details here," and most ominous, "have been told not to say anything important in case our letters go astray" (*OP* 8–9). What is going on?

~~~~~~~~~~~~~~~~~~~~~~~~~~

### LEFT IN THE DARK AND OUT IN THE COLD

Communication is very important to spies. Being able to talk to headquarters helps them to find out information, deliver it, and avoid discovery. As we all know, Dumbledore often leaves Harry in the dark, sometimes for good reasons—to let him make his own discoveries—but sometimes for the wrong reasons.

Spies with long-term assignments occasionally lose contact with headquarters, either to go deep undercover or because something has gone wrong. An agent left in the field with no communication from his or her handlers is said to be "out in the cold." When communication is restored, the agent has been "brought in from the cold." Lucius Malfoy was out in the cold for many years, but he is brought in from the cold after the Triwizard Tournament when Voldemort summons the Death Eaters through the Dark Mark.

As Harry learns later on, his friends have been told to limit what they write because the Order of the Phoenix is worried about secure communications. A secure line of communication, whether it involves written mail, phone and text conversations, email, instant messaging, or even speaking face to face, is critical for people who deal in secrets. After all, you don't want your adversary to intercept your messages.

In the Muggle world, spies use many different tools and techniques to keep communications secure. Agents often do not have the luxury of meeting in person with the case officer or members of their organization. The meeting could be observed and result in someone suspecting the spy. To avoid being observed, spies use "impersonal" forms of communication such as dead drops and brush passes, usually employing coded messages.

When communicating by telephone, it may be necessary to use an untraceable phone or one that can be used once and discarded. When communicating online, case officers might use special networks with enhanced security, or they might just send a one-way burst of information to headquarters.

When information must be exchanged in a physical form, such as photographs, maps, or paper documents, intelligence officers have the same problem that Harry and his friends did: It's relatively easy for the opposing side to catch covert messages exchanged via the post office or other mail and courier services. The most secret documents must be delivered from one person to another. That means arranging meetings that do not look like meetings at all. Or the agent (or case officer) might hide the documents at a prearranged location (dead drop) for the other person to pick up. Case officers are careful to make such contacts look like part of the agent's daily routine, so that nobody from the opposing side notes an unusual change in that agent's behavior.

## DEAD DROPS AND BRUSH CONTACTS

Precise communication is particularly important when a case officer employs *impersonal* communication techniques. One such technique is a *dead drop*, where the orders or other information are hidden in an agreed-upon location for later pickup.

Another way to pass information is using brush contacts, which take place when a case officer passes information to an agent (or vice versa) in a public place. The two individuals simply walk past each other and surreptitiously exchange the package. In such situations, the case officer and the agent have no chance to discuss details or answer questions. So, any messages exchanged in a dead drop or via brush contact must be carefully written – often in code – to be as clear as possible.

## TALKING IN CODE

Another way of securing communications is to make the information impossible for the other side to understand. This means sending a **coded message** within information that is unintelligible (or looks unimportant) to the opposing side. *Harry Potter and the Order of the Phoenix* has an excellent example of coded communication: the messages Harry sends to "Snuffles." Snuffles, of course, is the code name he and his friends have given to Sirius Black. Harry wants to send a message to Sirius by owl post, but he knows that Professor Umbridge and Filch have been reading students' mail. So Harry spends a lot of time considering how he will convey the essential information to Sirius without giving anything away— just in case somebody else should read it!

Harry starts by warning Sirius about his problems with Professor Umbridge in a way that no one but he and Sirius would understand: she is "nearly as nice as your mum." (The portrait of Sirius's mother at number twelve, Grimmauld Place, is *anything* but nice!) Then Harry writes, "That thing that I wrote to you about last summer happened again last night,"

meaning that his scar was hurting without Voldemort being near. He next says that he's missing "our biggest friend," a clear reference to Hagrid, who is not back yet from his mission for the Order. As Harry discovers, it takes a long time to write such a short letter because he must choose every word carefully, thinking about how Sirius—and most importantly someone else who intercepts the letter—will understand it, correctly or incorrectly.

In the same book, there is an example of using and breaking numeric codes. When Arthur Weasley takes Harry to the Ministry of Magic for his hearing, they enter the building through what appears to be a normal telephone box. Mr. Weasley dials the numbers 6-2-4-4-2, and the telephone box turns into an elevator to the Ministry's lobby. Harry remembers the code later for his unauthorized rescue mission. But what do the numbers mean? J. K. Rowling never tells us in the pages of her book, but we can do some spy work ourselves to figure it out!

One of the most basic forms of code involves substituting numbers for letters. For example, if you substitute 1 for *A*, 2 for *B*, and so on, you can write letters with numbers. Here is the code key for a direct substitution of numbers for letters:

| A | B | C | D | E | F | G | H | I | J | K | L | M |
|---|---|---|---|---|---|---|---|---|---|---|---|---|
| 1 | 2 | 3 | 4 | 5 | 6 | 7 | 8 | 9 | 10 | 11 | 12 | 13 |

| N | O | P | Q | R | S | T | U | V | W | X | Y | Z |
|---|---|---|---|---|---|---|---|---|---|---|---|---|
| 14 | 15 | 16 | 17 | 18 | 19 | 20 | 21 | 22 | 23 | 24 | 25 | 26 |

Using this code, you would write the message "Meet me tonight" like this:

| 13 | 5 | 5 | 20 | 13 | 5 | 20 | 15 | 14 | 9 | 7 | 8 | 20 |
|---|---|---|---|---|---|---|---|---|---|---|---|---|
| M | E | E | T | M | E | T | O | N | I | G | H | T |

If we apply this code to the Ministry of Magic code, what do we get?

| 6 | F |
|---|---|
| 2 | B |
| 4 | D |
| 4 | D |
| 2 | B |

F B D D B doesn't make much sense. Guess that must not be the correct way to break the code! Now, let's think like spies. Where are we? At the visitor's entrance to the Ministry of Magic. Check. What else?

We are in a *telephone* booth. Well, we know that there aren't enough numbers in Mr. Weasley's code to be a phone number. In London, home to Ministry of Magic headquarters, telephone numbers have ten digits. However, anyone who has sent a text message using the keys on a cell phone knows that there's another code in place. Eight of the nine number keys on a standard phone have letters on them as well.

## 6-2-4-4-2

What happens if we use those numbers instead of a direct number-for-letter substitution? We get three letters for each number by looking at the phone numbers and the letters that relate to each number:

6 M N O
2 A B C
4 G H I
4 G H I
2 A B C

See anything?

6 **M** N O
2 **A** B C
4 **G** H I
4 G H **I**
2 A B **C**

**MAGIC!**

J. K. Rowling never tells us how to break the code, but by using logic we have decoded the password for the Ministry of Magic visitor's entrance!

# SECURING SECRETS

Once an organization has acquired secret information, it wants to keep that information safe from prying eyes. Keeping information secure involves many levels of precautions, from training people to keep their knowledge safe, to authorizing only certain people to access secret information, to creating highly secure physical spaces for storing and discussing secret information. All of these precautions control just who it is that has access to secure information.

~~~~~~~~~~~~~~~~~~~~~~~~~~~~~~~~~~~~~~~

## BIGOT LISTS

The fewer the people who know a secret, the less likely it is to be exposed. Knowledge of the location of the Order of the Phoenix's headquarters and access to it are limited strictly to those who have a *need to know*. A list of people who have been given such highly secret information is called a *bigot list*. The term comes from World War II, when the British armed forces created a top-secret plan to attack the German forces occupying France: a **B**ritish **I**nvasion of **G**erman **O**ccupied **T**erritory. The few English and American officers who had access to and knowledge of the date and location of the Normandy Invasion were thus on the BIGOT list.

An example of limiting information only to those who need to know is the Order of the Phoenix meetings, where only the adults are allowed into the meeting and Harry and his friends are kept out. The Weasley twins use their Extendable Ears to try to listen to the meeting, but Mrs. Weasley use a counterjinx (countermeasure) to prevent them from being able to listen to what is being said.

All spies know that people—and sometimes technology—are the weakest link in any organizations. Members of intelligence organizations learn to be careful with the information in their care. Persons in the spy world must think before they make even the most casual comment. All intelligence officers must remember to put away any sensitive documents before walking away from their desks, so that people who walk past don't have the chance to peek at them. Intelligence officers must agree not to talk with other people about their work—not even with their spouses or best friends—because there's a chance that seemingly innocent chat might put information into the wrong hands.

For example, think about how many times Hagrid gets into trouble because he can't stop talking about the secret work he does for Dumbledore. In the first book, he accidentally tells a disguised Professor Quirrell how to get past Fluffy, the three-headed dog that guards the Philosopher's Stone. When Hagrid is questioned, whether by Professor Umbridge or Harry and his friends, he almost always lets critical information slip— he's terrible at hiding the truth. A responsible intelligence officer would never share information with friends as easily as Hagrid confides in Harry, Hermione, and Ron!

Intelligence agencies also use passwords and security questions to keep information secret. A password is a secret string of letters and numbers that only you should know. A strong password is one that is not easy to guess: a password like *123456* or *passw0rd*, for instance, is easier to guess than a nonsensical string of characters like Hp1mfbc3.

(By the way, that nonsensical string is based on a code! The key phrase is "**H**arry **P**otter **is** **m**y **f**avorite **b**ook **c**haracter **e**ver," with the number 1 substituted for letter *l* and the number 3 substituted for the letter *e*.)

Harry uses passwords every day at Hogwarts. He needs one to get into Gryffindor tower, and that password changes regularly, making it hard for others to learn and use it. The door to the Headmaster's office also requires a password— though once Harry realizes that Dumbledore uses the names of candies for his passwords, it's not hard for him to guess the correct one!

If you have ever forgotten your login name or password for a website, then you probably know about security questions, too. When you set up an account online, you provide answers to questions that only you should know, like, *What is the name of your first pet?* or *What was the name of your favorite teacher?* The answers are things that strangers would not know about you, and that shouldn't be easy to guess from your social media postings or publicly available information.

At the beginning of *Harry Potter and the Order of the Phoenix*, Mad-Eye Moody is worried that Voldemort's forces might be using Polyjuice Potion to impersonate members of the Order and infiltrate the organization. He even suspects Harry as being fake! So, when the Order arrives at the Dursleys' house to bring Harry to headquarters, Lupin asks Harry a security question: "What form does your Patronus take?" Harry of course answers correctly, "A stag," and the Order members agree that it must be him.

Now, let's do a little bit of thinking about Mad-Eye's security question, like a good intelligence officer. Was that a good security question? Is it something that the opposing side might guess or find out through research? In choosing the question to be asked, the security officer should consider who else knows what form Harry's Patronus takes. Lupin taught Harry the spell, so he knows the form it takes—but Lupin is a member of the Order and therefore trustworthy. Harry has told his friends Ron and Hermione about what his Patronus looks like, but they, too, can be trusted.

However, in *Harry Potter and the Prisoner of Azkaban*, when Draco Malfoy, Crabbe, and Goyle dress up as Dementors to distract Harry during a Quidditch match, Harry thinks they are real dementors and casts a fully formed Patronus at them—*in front of an entire stadium of Quidditch fans.* Not only is it likely that every student and professor at Hogwarts saw the form of Harry's Patronus, but his arch-rival Draco Malfoy very certainly saw it. Draco could have easily told his father that Harry's Patronus is a stag. So, for all Mad-Eye Moody's precautions, that particular choice of security question wasn't the best! It's just one example of how easy it is for human error to foil the most careful security plans.

## SECURITY CLEARANCES

Access to secure information is controlled by the use of security **clearances**, which are formal levels of access, awarded by the government, that allow a person access to restricted information.

The most basic clearance is Confidential: a person with that level of clearance can access classified information secured at the Confidential level. The next level is Secret, and the level after that is Top Secret. At the very highest level of security, Top Secret information is placed into special compartments—literally boxed up—in a place that only a select few people can enter. This highest level of classified material is called Sensitive Compartmented Information, or SCI. The place where such information is kept is called a **sensitive compartmented information facility, or SCIF**. In many cases, it is simply a large vault, like the ones used by banks. People with proper clearance use a computer—one that is connected only to other secure computers—to review the highly classified information. A SCIF might also be a special room protected from all forms of eavesdropping, so that people with the proper clearance may talk without fear of being overheard.

## COUNTERINTELLIGENCE

**Counterintelligence** is protecting secrets by looking for spies inside the organization (moles) or protecting the organization from persons trying to get inside the organization. Hermione casts spells around the tent while the trio is on the run in *Harry Potter and the Deathly Hallows*. These spells are used to hide our friends from the people (Snatchers) who are looking for them. The Department of Mysteries also has numerous protections preventing witches and wizards from gaining access to that area or getting ahold of a Prophecy.

Counterintelligence is used to find moles or security risks

within an organization. Just as there's no easy way for a wizard or witch to identify whether a friend or colleague is acting under an Imperius Curse, it's hard for Muggle intelligence officers to know whether someone in their organization has been turned, either willingly or through blackmail. If an agent who has been recruited falls under suspicion, his or her case officer might begin a quiet investigation to find out whether that person has been acting suspiciously or has done something that might be used to force the agent to spy for the other side.

When Harry, Ron, and Hermione arrive at the Lovegoods' home in *Harry Potter and the Deathly Hallows,* for instance, Xenophilius Lovegood acts very strangely. The trio soon learns that the Death Eaters have kidnapped Luna and threatened to kill her if Xenophilius does not turn on Harry and take the side of the Ministry in his magazine, *The Quibbler.*

## PROPAGANDA AND DISINFORMATION

Propaganda is information distributed to influence people or governments. It can be either positive or negative information. It may be accurate, or false. **Disinformation**, which is a form of propaganda, is deliberately inaccurate. Normally, disinformation is disseminated by a government or an organization to mislead or deceive its adversaries or even its own citizens.

In *Harry Potter and the Order of the Phoenix,* the *Daily Prophet* runs a disinformation campaign to make Harry look bad. In article after article, the paper describes Harry alternately as hungry for fame, a pawn of Dumbledore's political ambitions, a clueless child, and even mentally ill—all without letting Harry defend himself. This disinformation creates doubt about Harry Potter in the minds of everyone who reads it, which makes it very hard for Harry to find friends and allies or convince people of the danger of Voldemort's imminent return.

Later in the same book, Voldemort uses the mysterious connection between himself and Harry to deliver some very convincing disinformation campaign. In one of his visions, Harry sees Sirius being tortured by Voldemort in the Department of Mysteries. Hermione (who would make an exceptional intelligence analyst) asks Harry whether the vision might in fact be fake. But Harry lets emotion override common sense and races off to the Ministry of Magic to save his godfather—only to fall right into Voldemort's trap. Disinformation can be very powerful!

The *Daily Prophet*'s disinformation campaign is properly considered *propaganda*. Propaganda is where a government spreads ideas and statements to support a particular cause or viewpoint. The Ministry is using propaganda in the same way that many Muggle governments have done in the past. Unfortunately, some governments exercise control over what is reported by their own countries' major media sources (such as television stations, newspapers, and Internet services) to drown out or discredit opponents. This is exactly what the Ministry of Magic does relating to Harry Potter.

It is important for spies and citizens alike to be able to identify propaganda and seek out unbiased information. In 2010, during the series of revolutionary protests and demonstrations known as the Arab Spring, citizens of countries with government-controlled media used smartphones and a variety of social media services to find and exchange information and organize resistance. In turn, intelligence officers from around the world gathered information from these informal unofficial communications in order to find out what was really happening in these countries and to judge the potential actions (or even disintegration) of the governing organizations.

Spreading disinformation can also serve as an active form of counterintelligence that works to confuse anyone who happens to be spying on you. Disinformation is information that is not true. When an intelligence agency intentionally spreads untrue information, it can confuse the other side and cause them to report incorrect information to their organization.

## COUNTERMEASURES

Another part of counterintelligence is *countermeasures,* the devices and actions used to prevent someone from observing or discovering another person's activities. In *Harry Potter and the Order of the Phoenix,* for example, Molly Weasley knows that Fred and George plan to use their Extendable Ears, a long-distance

listening device, to spy on the Order's meetings. She takes countermeasures by casting an Imperturbable Charm on the kitchen door, blocking the ability of the Weasley twins to listen to the Order of the Phoenix meetings.

The Wizarding world has also created many useful tools to detect spying or other threats. Mad-Eye Moody has a large collection of Dark Detectors, devices that alert the owner to the presence of Dark Magic. His Secrecy Sensor, as described in *Harry Potter and the Goblet of Fire*, vibrates when it detects someone lying or hiding something. (Of course, at the moment Harry sees the device, it is vibrating madly because the real Professor Moody has been imprisoned, and Harry is really talking to Barty Crouch Jr. in disguise. The false Professor Moody explains it away by claiming that it has detected too many students lying about their homework.)

When Harry reserves the Room of Requirement for study sessions for Dumbledore's Army, the room appears with many different kinds of Dark Detectors, including Sneakoscopes. The Sneakoscope looks like a glass top, and it spins, lights up, and whistles whenever someone does something untrustworthy near it. Ron and Hermione both give Harry pocket Sneako-scopes as gifts—which turn out to be useful, though they can only signal the presence of sneaky behavior and not the identity of the person doing the sneaking.

Although Muggle spies don't have anything as flashy as spinning, screeching Sneakoscopes, they do have sophisticated motion sensors, camera systems, and digital security programs that *quietly* alert counterintelligence officers when people are poking around in places they shouldn't be.

Muggles also use lie-detecting devices instead of Sneakoscopes, the most common being the **polygraph** test. A polygraph is a device that measures a person's bodily reactions, such as blood pressure, pulse, and breathing rate. While a person is connected to the polygraph, an examiner asks very detailed questions, and the device records even the slightest changes in that person's physical state. If the person tells a lie, the device records signs of anxiety, such as a faster heartbeat or increased sweating.

Extendable Ears and Dark Detectors are fantastic countermeasures for people who can use magic. Muggle spies use some amazing tools as well. In the next chapter, we'll look at the clever gadgets spies use, as well as the skills that good spies use to practice their craft.

# CHAPTER 3
# ACTIVITIES

# 3·1. MAZE

Help the **Gray Lady** Reach the **Ravenclaw** Common Room!

## 3·2. BREAKING THE CODE – HELP HARRY FIND WHAT HE IS LOOKING FOR (HORCRUXES)

| | | |
|---|---|---|
| A – U | J – D | S – M |
| B – V | K – E | T – N |
| C – W | L – F | U – O |
| D – X | M – G | V – P |
| E – Y | N – H | W – Q |
| F – Z | O – I | X – R |
| G – A | P – J | Y – S |
| H – B | Q – K | Z – T |
| I – C | R – L | |

1. Z U S    X O J J R K 'Y    J O G X E

2. S G X B U R U    M G A T Z 'Y    X O T M

3. Y G R G F G X    Y R E Z N K X O T 'Y

R U I Q K Z

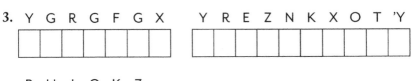

| | | |
|---|---|---|
| A – U | J – D | S – M |
| B – V | K – E | T – N |
| C – W | L – F | U – O |
| D – X | M – G | V – P |
| E – Y | N – H | W – Q |
| F – Z | O – I | X – R |
| G – A | P – J | Y – S |
| H – B | Q – K | Z – T |
| I – C | R – L | |

**4.** N  K  R  M  G     N  A  L  L  R  K  V  A  L  L  'Y

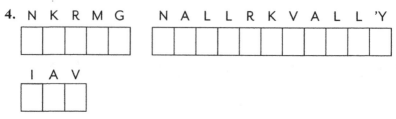

I  A  V

**5.** X  U  C  K  T  G     X  G  B  K  T  I  R  G  C  'Y

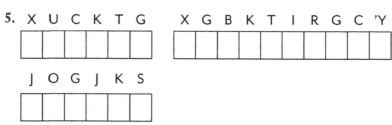

J  O  G  J  K  S

**6.** T  G  M  O  T  O

# 3·3. MATCHING – MATCH THE YULE-BALL DATES

Draw a line from the boy to his date at the Yule Ball in *Harry Potter and the Goblet of Fire.*

Fred Weasley (*GF* 394)                      Fleur Delacour

Cedric Diggory  (*GF* 397)                   Ginny Weasley

Seamus Finnigan (*GF* 401)                  Pansy Parkinson

Harry Potter (*GF* 401)                      Parvati Patil

Neville Longbottom (*GF* 401)               Cho Chang

Ron Weasley (*GF* 402, 412)                 Hermione Granger

Roger Davies (*GF* 412–13)                  Padma Patil

Draco Malfoy (*GF* 413)                     Lavender Brown

Viktor Krum (*GF* 414)                      Angelina Johnson

# 3·4. MATCHING – SPY TERMS IN THE HARRY POTTER SERIES FOR FIFTH YEARS

Match the word with the term by putting the number of the term in the blank.

**17. agent provocateur**      _____ An individual who serves as a catalyst to get others to take actions. *Example:* Lee Jordan was trying to provoke Professor Umbridge by placing nifflers in her office.

**18. cell**      _____ A false story that provides an alternative for the truth, intended to conceal an agent's true reasons for being being in a particular place. *Example:* The Dursleys tell their neighbors that Harry is gone during the school year because he is attending St. Brutus's Secure Center for Incurably Criminal Boys.

**19. cover story**      _____ A group that is working together on a combined project or mission. *Example:* Dumbledore's Army is a group of students assembled to practice Defense Against the Dark Arts.

**20. deep cover**      _____ A mission or assignment so secret that only one or two people know of its existence. *Example:* No one knows about Snape's role spying on Voldemort except Dumbledore.

# 3·5. CROSSWORD – HARRY POTTER SPIES AND OPERATIVES

## ACROSS

2. The initials of the person who left a note in the locket

4. Something used to gain access to a place, such as "Lemon Drop"

8. The inventors of the Extendable Ears (3 words)

11. Snape's handler

# DOWN

1. The person who is able to see what Voldemort is doing (2 words)

3. Voldemort's assistant and spy in book 1

5. The double agent who spies on Voldemort throughout the series

6. The member of the DA who suggests using Thestrals to fly to the Ministry of Magic

7. The device invented by Hermione to tell DA members when the next meeting will occur

9. The name Harry calls his godfather Sirius in his open-code letter to him

10. An electronic listening device, or Rita Skeeter

# 3.6. FILL IN THE BLANK – THE LIFE OF J. K. ROWLING (THE MIDDLE YEARS) – PART 3

How well do you know Jo? Here is your chance to discover the details of her life and the sources of many of the Harry Potter characters. Just fill in the blank, if you can!

21. Jo spends six years working mostly secretarial jobs, including two years for _____ _____ investigating human rights violations in Africa. *Hint: They investigate such violations all over the world, thus the second word.*

    **21. Answer:** _____ _____

22. She takes a job with The Manchester Chamber of Commerce, commuting to work via, you guessed it, a

    _____.

    **22. Answer:** _____

23. While coming back from Manchester in 1990, there are mechanical problems that result in a delay of four hours. While stuck and looking at a group of cows, Jo has a sudden idea for the Harry Potter story and has the basic premise written in her mind by the time she arrives at _____ _____ station. *Hint: The Hogwarts Express leaves from here.*

    **23. Answer:** _____ _____

24. Jo's mother is diagnosed with _____ _____, and dies soon thereafter at age forty-five. *Hint: It goes by the letters "MS."*

    **24. Answer:** _____ _____

**25.** Jo takes a position in Oporto, Portugal, teaching _____ as a second language afternoons and evenings, and writing in the mornings. *Hint:* Les Misérables.

**25. Answer:** _____

**26.** After a very short whirlwind courtship, Jo gets married to a television _____. *Hint: He would need to be a writer too.*

**26. Answer:** _____

**27.** After about two years of marriage, _____ is born, but shortly thereafter Jo gets divorced and returns to Great Britain.

**27. Answer:** _____

**28.** Jo and her daughter move in to Jo's sister's home in Edinburgh, the capital of _____. *Hint: Best to wear a kilt.*

**28. Answer:** _____

**29.** Jo reads the first _____ chapters of Harry Potter to her sister, who likes it; as a result, Jo decides to continue working on it.

**29. Answer:** _____

**30.** Jo takes one year "off" in Edinburgh to write the first Potter book, strolling Jessica around until she falls asleep, often writing in her favorite place, Nicolson's _____ and The Elephant House. *Hint: It's not a pub but a small place to eat adjacent to the street.*

**30. Answer:** _____

## 3-7. FILL IN THE BLANK – THE LIFE OF SEVERUS SNAPE (DOUBLE AGENT) – PART 3

**16.** Snape meets with Dumbledore on top of a _____ and asks Dumbledore to hide the Potters, hide them all, to keep them safe; in return, Snape promises Dumbledore "_____" (*DH* 677).

**16. Answers:** _____ and _____

**17.** Snape meets with Dumbledore after Lily and James's death and is told that the boy lived; Snape agrees to help protect _____'s _____ but insists that Dumbledore "never—never tell" (*DH* 679).

**17. Answer :** _____'s _____

**18.** Snape begins teaching at Hogwarts, though he is not allowed to teach the course he wants to teach, _____ _____ _____ _____ (five words) until year 6 (*SS* 126; *OP* 363 ; *HBP* 166).

**18. Answers:** _____ _____ _____ _____ _____

**19.** Snape complains to Dumbledore about Harry during Harry's first year, and during this discussion Dumbledore asks Snape to keep an eye on Professor _____ (*DH* 679).

**19. Answer:** _____

**20.** Snape's Dark Mark becomes darker during Harry's fourth year; the Durmstrang Headmaster ＿＿＿＿＿ intends to flee, but Snape will remain (*DH* 679).

**20. Answer:** ＿＿＿＿＿

**21.** Snape ignores the Dark Mark when it returns, but goes to the Dark Lord ＿＿＿＿＿ hours later on ＿＿＿＿＿'s orders, convinces Voldemort that he has remained faithful, and provides Voldemort ＿＿＿＿＿ years of information on Dumbledore (*GF* 709–10, 713; *HBP* 28–29).

**21. Answers:**

＿＿＿＿＿＿＿＿＿＿＿＿＿

＿＿＿＿＿＿＿＿＿＿＿＿＿

＿＿＿＿＿＿＿＿＿＿＿＿＿

# CHAPTER 3

# ANSWERS

## 3·1. ANSWERS TO MAZE – HELP THE GRAY LADY FIND THE RAVENCLAW COMMON ROOM

## 3.2. ANSWERS TO BREAKING THE CODE – HELP HARRY FIND WHAT HE IS LOOKING FOR [HORCRUXES]:

1. TOM RIDDLE'S DIARY
2. MARVOLO GAUNT'S RING
3. SALAZAR SLYTHERIN'S LOCKET
4. HELGA HUFFLEPUFF'S CUP
5. ROWENA RAVENCLAW'S DIADEM
6. NAGINI

## 3.3. ANSWERS TO MATCHING – MATCH THE YULE BALL DATES:

Fred Weasley (*GF* 394) . . . . . . . . . . Angelina Johnson
Cedric Diggory (*GF* 397) . . . . . . . . . . . . . Cho Chang
Seamus Finnigan (*GF* 401) . . . . . . . . Lavender Brown
Harry Potter (*GF* 401) . . . . . . . . . . . . . . Parvati Patil
Neville Longbottom (*GF* 401) . . . . . . Ginny Weasley
Ron Weasley (*GF* 402, 412) . . . . . . . . . . . Padma Patil
Roger Davies (*GF* 412–13) . . . . . . . . Fleur Delacour
Draco Malfoy (*GF* 413) . . . . . . . . . . Pansy Parkinson
Viktor Krum (*GF* 414) . . . . . . . . . Hermione Granger

## 3.4. ANSWERS TO MATCHING – SPY TERMS IN THE HARRY POTTER SERIES FOR FIFTH YEARS

17 agent provocateur, 19 cover story, 18 cell, and 20 deep cover

# 3.5. ANSWERS TO CROSSWORD – HARRY POTTER SPIES AND OPERATIVES:

**Across**
- 2. RAB
- 4. PASSWORD
- 8. THE WEASLEY TWINS
- 11. DUMBLEDORE

**Down**
- 1. HARRY POTTER
- 3. QUIRRELL
- 5. SNAPE
- 6. LUNA
- 7. COIN
- 9. SNUFFLES
- 10. BUG

# 3.6. ANSWERS TO FILL IN THE BLANK – THE LIFE OF J. K. ROWLING (THE MIDDLE YEARS) – PART 3

- 21. Amnesty International
- 22. train
- 23. King's Cross
- 24. multiple sclerosis
- 25. English
- 26. journalist
- 27. Jessica
- 28. Scotland
- 29. three
- 30. café

## 3.7. ANSWERS TO THE LIFE OF SEVERUS SNAPE (DOUBLE AGENT) – PART 3

16. hill, anything
17. Lily's son
18. Defense Against the Dark Arts
19. Quirrell
20. Karkaroff
21. two, Dumbledore's, sixteen

# Chapter 4

## SPYCRAFT

The Weird Sisters

When you add up all of the skills and tools needed to make an excellent case officer, you get what's known as **spycraft**, called tradecraft in the intelligence world. Spycraft includes the ability to use spy tools, such as bugs, disguises, and weapons, as well as the ability to gather and analyze information, to access secure locations, to communicate securely, and perhaps most importantly, to understand opponents and use that understanding against them.

## HUMINT AND PROPHECIES

Human intelligence—that is, information received from people—is often the most essential information obtained, and the most dubious. The quality of the information depends on the person giving it and the source of that person's knowledge. Spies and agents discover important facts, but also information on the capabilities and intentions of the organization or government that is targeted. Information gathered by spies is often used to provide estimates or predictions, including predictions on what a certain leader or country will do. Thus, factual information is often used to try to determine what might happen in the future.

In the world of Harry Potter, essential information has been provided by prophecies. Sybill Trelawney provides the original prophecy to Albus Dumbledore regarding a child born at the end of July that will defeat the Dark Lord, and she also provides a later prophecy about the return of Voldemort.

Although it is easy for Muggles to discount the idea of prophecies, in reality intelligence analysts do just that: they provide prophecies based on real-world information and the application of both **psychological assessments** and intelligence analysis. Muggles have considered the importance of prophecies from the time they began thinking, talking, and then writing about the future. The Bible, the Koran, the Torah, and even great works of literature (such as Homer's *Iliad* and *Odyssey*) are filled with prophecies. And which prophecy in Muggle literature finds itself intertwined with the world of Harry Potter, and is perhaps the basis of J. K. Rowling's use of prophecies? The three witches in *Macbeth*! (By the way, do you happen to know the name of the rock band that plays at Nearly Headless Nick's Death Party? *The Weird Sisters*, which just happens to be what Macbeth constantly calls the three witches!)

## SPECTACULAR SPY GADGETS

When you watch a James Bond movie, you probably look forward to seeing what amazing new gadgets he uses on his mission. Bond's tools are just as amazing as many of the magical devices in the world of Harry Potter.

We already mentioned Fred and George Weasley's clever Extendable Ears, which look like long, flesh-colored pieces of string. If you stick one end in your ear and get the other end close to the people you want to listen in on, you can hear anything they say as clearly as if you were standing right next to them. And Rita Skeeter, as an unregistered Animagus, can turn into a beetle and sneak around unnoticed, listening to private conversations.

Muggle spies listen in on opponents' conversations by

planting electronic bugs, which are small devices that are secretly placed at a target's home or office and used to record or broadcast all sounds made in that space—conversations, phone calls, and even sounds of office cleaning staff or household pets (which is called the "take").

～～～～～～～～～～～～～～～～

## BUGGING A DESK

When Peter was working in the intelligence world, he suspected that one of his sources was working for the opposing side. Peter set out to bug the source's office and find out how many other organizations the man reported to.

The source was a man who liked holding dinner parties at his home, and soon he invited Peter and his wife to a casual gathering. Before Peter and his wife left for the party, Peter strapped a bug to his leg. The bug was a slender, foot-long piece of wood with a microphone and a radio transmitter attached to it, along with batteries to power the device. Peter asked his wife to wait until he excused himself from the party to use the bathroom, and then to keep the host distracted with conversation until he returned. Peter had visited the townhouse before, so he knew that there was a bathroom on the lower level—near the source's personal office.

Peter slipped away from the party, went downstairs to the source's office, and used a silent drill to install the bug in the space between the back of a drawer and the rear panel of the source's desk. He was careful to collect the sawdust created by the drilling and hide it in his pocket, so that there was no sign of what he'd done. Peter turned the bug on and quietly rejoined the party.

In the next few weeks, Peter monitored the source's conversations, and sure enough, the man was working for multiple intelligence organizations. Peter fired the source—but he didn't give a reason for it, so the source never knew that he'd been bugged!

If it's not possible to plant a bug in an opponent's territory, spies can also use long-distance devices to listen in on the target's activities. Tools such as laser microphones and parabolic dishes zoom in on a distant place and transmit all sounds from it back to the listener.

## HOW TO DEFEAT A LASER MIC

While Lynn was visiting the **National Security Agency (NSA)**, he talked with a former CIA scientist about an imaginary challenge: defeating a laser microphone aimed at the window of his cabin in Montana. A laser mic records the vibrations of people's voices in a window or other reflective surface and converts them to audio signal for eavesdroppers.

The scientist suggested that Lynn could defeat the laser microphone by surrounding the window with copper wiring (at a cost of hundreds of thousands of dollars). However, a cheaper and easier solution, the two decided, would be a motorized device that taps at the window at about one thousand beats per second. The motorized tapping would create a new vibration pattern on the windows and interrupt any vibrations created by people talking inside the house. While Lynn might not be doing any spy work in his cabin, intelligence officers must be thinking of such counterintelligence measures at all times in order to keep their work hidden.

---

Spy tools also help intelligence officers to communicate in secret. Magic users have many ways of communicating without leaving a trace, whether they use the Floo Network to chat face to face or send messages by Patronus, as Kingsley Shacklebolt does during Bill and Fleur's wedding in *Harry Potter and the Deathly Hallows*. Wizards and witches also use spells to secure written communications, as Hermione does when she jinxes the list of members of Dumbledore's Army to identify anyone who broke the agreement to keep it secret. Perhaps the most wonderful bit of secret writing is the Marauder's Map, which shows itself only to those who know the password spell . . . and insults anyone else who tries to read it!

Muggle spies can't use magic to deliver messages, but they do take precautions to secure written communications. Spies have used invisible ink to deliver written messages for centuries. One of the simplest invisible inks is lemon juice mixed with water, which dries clear on paper but appears again when

the paper is heated. Lemon juice was used for spy communications as late as World War I (1914–1918). But such old-fashioned techniques were easy for the opposition to spot, so intelligence experts developed complicated chemical inks that required exposure to ultraviolet light, steaming with iodine, or bathing in special chemicals before reading. Today, invisible inks are more likely to be dried chemicals that the case officer or agent rubs onto a sheet of paper before writing down crucial information. Muggle spies also use special papers for covert communication, including paper that dissolves in water, and flash paper, which disappears completely when set on fire, leaving no ashes behind.

Hermione's charmed coins that she creates for the members of Dumbledore's Army in *Harry Potter and the Order of the Phoenix* are especially clever communication devices. Harry holds a master coin (a Galleon) on which he marks the date and time of the next DA gathering. When he has updated the information, the dates on the rest of the coins change to match, and the coins heat up to let the other members of Dumbledore's Army know of the change.

Coins have been used in the Muggle world as well. During the Cold War, Soviet spies used a U.S. nickel with a hollow core to carry messages written on microfilm that had extremely small writing that could be magnified and read. This method of communication was uncovered when a Soviet spy accidentally "spent" the nickel and it was eventually given to a young newspaper delivery boy to pay for a subscription. The young boy told a young girl about it, and she told her father, who was a policeman, who told a detective, who alerted the FBI. (You can see a similar nickel at the International Spy Museum today!)

## DISGUISES: DISAPPEARING IN PLAIN SIGHT

Disguising oneself is much easier for the wizards and witches of Harry Potter's world than it is in the Muggle world. An Animagus like Professor McGonagall or Sirius Black can turn into an animal at will, and a Metamorphmagus such as Tonks can change his or her appearance just by thinking about it. In the Wizarding world those who aren't born with those skills can still use Polyjuice Potion to impersonate someone else. And, of course, there's always Harry's amazing Invisibility Cloak, which hides its wearer completely from view.

But even witches and wizards sometimes hide behind nothing more than clothing. In *Harry Potter and the Order of the Phoenix,* Mundungus Fletcher eavesdrops on the organizational meeting of Dumbledore's Army while disguised as a veiled witch. And whenever witches and wizards go out into the Muggle world, they dress up as Muggles—or at least what they *think* Muggles look like—in order to blend in and not violate the Statute of Secrecy.

Muggles are known to employ complicated disguises using masks, makeup, wigs, and costumes to infiltrate enemy territory, as shown in James Bond and the spies of the TV and film series *Mission: Impossible.* Some disguises even aim to make a human look like part of the landscape: a spy approaching an isolated location might use a disguise made of tree branches and leaves to blend in with the surrounding plant life (called camouflage).

Muggle spies also use uncomplicated disguises and regular clothing, because the object is to *blend in* with what observers *expect* to see. If a case officer is breaking into an office, she or he might dress in business clothing to match the other employees of that company, or in the uniform of a cleaning or maintenance service that regularly works in the building. A disguise might change something as subtle as the way you walk, how straight you stand, or simply the addition of a hat and mustache.

While spies in the Muggle world don't have Invisibility Cloaks yet, they are developing technology that comes pretty close to it. Certain military planes and ships use so-called "stealth" technologies to make them almost invisible to radar and other long-distance sensing devices, although they are still visible to the eye. Certain reflective fabrics can mimic the area around them, creating "camouflage" for whatever— or whoever—is beneath them. And scientists are working on surface films that divert rays of light, making it impossible to see what's underneath.

## IT'S ALL IN YOUR HEAD

While intelligence officers may use high-tech tools and clever disguises to get their work done, their most important skills are mental, such as analytical skills, foreign language ability, memory, **observation**, and quick thinking. A good spy develops certain habits or traits that are important to all espionage work, whether they use them on field assignments or in analysis or while planning missions.

Staying cool and keeping your wits about you is one of the important traits of a spy. It's the ability to choose the best actions at all times, even under great stress. When superior officers accused Polish spy Colonel Kuklinski, along with two other officers, of stealing information, he didn't panic. When the other two officers claimed innocence, Kuklinski did as well. Thinking quickly, he pointed out that another group of people also had access to the stolen information. He successfully shifted suspicion—at least for the moment—away from himself and, soon afterward, escaped to the United States with his family.

Harry Potter, on a few occasions, is not always good at keeping his cool. At the beginning of *Harry Potter and the Order of the Phoenix,* Dudley mocks him for having nightmares, and Harry loses his temper and whips out his wand, threatening to use magic even though it's illegal for him to do so outside of Hogwarts. Later on in the same book, Harry gets into even more trouble when, faced with insults and taunting from Slytherin House, he and George Weasley are goaded into a fistfight with Draco Malfoy. Dolores Umbridge takes this as a chance to ban both boys from Quidditch, teaching Harry a valuable lesson about keeping his cool.

Another good spy trait is the ability to take quick and decisive action. There are various ways to try to train a person to learn to act quickly and decisively. For example, Air Force pilots have been taught something called the OODA loop, which refers to the decision cycle of Observe, Orient, Decide, and Act. This concept was created by Col. John Boyd for military fighter pilots, though this method can easily apply to anyone who is trying to learn to make fast but good decisions.

Another crucial spy skill is the power of observation. Important information about a place or the people who occupy it can be gleaned by using all five senses to observe a scene and then taking care to form accurate memories about that sensory information. Good spies must always be aware of what is going on around them. They must quickly differentiate between

important and unimportant data. Trained case officers take in all sorts of information as they observe a location or another person, filing away as much as possible for later analysis. Much of this information won't be relevant, but small details can help in planning and executing missions: the location of a back door, for instance, or the time at which the mail is usually delivered to a particular location. A good spy can also determine whether something that *looks* unimportant really is important. Little details that seem unimportant at the time may turn out to be important indeed!

## SITUATIONAL AWARENESS

The ability to perceive the important things all around you is called **situational awareness** or *heightened awareness*. For example, military pilots are trained to pay attention to everything around them, at all times, so they don't run into each other while flying in close formation. Harry Potter has amazing skills in situational awareness: During the average Quidditch game, he must know where all of his teammates are, where the members of the opposing team are, and whether a Bludger is on his tail, all the while keeping an eye out for the Snitch. And because he's flying, he must look not only to his front and back, left and right, but also above and below his position.

Spies, too, learn to be attuned to everything around them. (It's too bad that they can't use Quidditch as a training exercise!) If someone walks up to you very quietly, you need to know they're there. If you're acting as a bodyguard, you must be aware of potential threats all around the person you're protecting, even above and below your **asset**. If somebody is following you, you need to be aware of it—but without just turning around and looking. Windows, mirrors, and even hubcaps can be used to "see" as if you have eyes in the back of your head— just like Mad-Eye Moody!

~~~~~~~~~~~~~~~~~~~~~~~~~~~~~~~~~~~~~~

A good example of noticing (and recalling) something that initially seems unimportant occurs in *Harry Potter and the Deathly Hallows*, where Harry notices—thanks in part to his observation of Viktor Krum's reaction to it—Mr. Lovegood's necklace, which bears a symbol that Harry doesn't recognize (Deathly Hallows). Hermione later notices the same symbol on Ignotus Peverell's gravestone and makes an important connection. They remember this information and realize it is important. They therefore visit Mr. Lovegood and receive an explanation of the Deathly Hallows, which helps them figure out their next step. In the same book, Harry and his friends remember another important detail: the presence of a very old-looking locket in a cabinet at the Black family home that they were unable to open. That clue—recalled two years later—leads them to finding one of the Horcruxes!

## KIM'S GAME

Another story about an orphan boy who learns spycraft is Rudyard Kipling's *Kim* (1901). Growing up in British-ruled India in the nineteenth century, Kim is befriended by a spy who is working for the British and trains in secret to spy on the Russians who are trying to gain influence in India. One of his teachers sharpens Kim's powers of observation by showing him a tray of jewels and other objects and then covering the tray with paper. Kim must then make a list of everything on the tray. Later, the teacher adds or removes objects from the tray, and Kim lists what has changed. This method of developing powers of observation is still known as "Kim's Game."

~~~~~~~~~~~~~~~~~~~~~~~~~~~~~~

Another important tool in the spy business is understanding how people think and make decisions. Spies learn to evaluate people and their patterns of behavior, which is called psychological assessment. Case officers use this ability on many people: persons they want to recruit, the leaders of foreign countries, and their intelligence sources.

This might seem like an easy skill to learn, but intelligence officers must first learn to overcome the urge to make decisions based on assumptions and biases. Assumptions are facts or statements that you take for granted. If you're planning a mission in a popular vacation spot, for instance, you might assume that the weather will be pleasant. What will happen if a major storm happens to hit while you're there? Will your assumptions leave you unprepared?

Biases can also be derived from particular kinds of assumptions we make about other people. One negative bias is a tendency to believe that certain ideas, beliefs, or even people are automatically better (or worse) than others, or have specific traits that apply to the whole group. This is sometimes called inherent bias. Such biases often lead to unfair treatment of the person or people thought to have these general characteristics. A biased person judges others based on a perception, often a negative one, of how they act, what they believe, or even how they look. Biases can also be helpful—think of all the times Harry avoids getting expelled because the professors like him! But biases and other forms of prejudice more often lead to someone being treated unfairly.

Harry and Professor Snape are each biased against the other. And many characters, even some well-meaning ones, are biased against Hagrid because they think his giant blood makes him stupid or violent, or that his generous heart makes him naïve. Bias has made it hard for Hagrid to get a job, make friends, and otherwise live a happy life.

When performing a psychological assessment of another person, an intelligence officer must always be aware not only of the biases that have affected that person and the biases that person holds, but also of any assumptions and biases the intelligence officer has about that person.

It's very dangerous to make assumptions, especially the type where another person or group of people is deemed worthless or less than human. During World War II, such assumptions led to the death of millions of people in German concentration camps. Bias also played a part when the U.S. government, claiming a safety concern, used bias and prejudice to justify the imprisonment of more than 120,000 Japanese Americans in internment camps for the duration of the war. When those in power portray a person or group of people as less than human, it is easier for the majority to accept unfair treatment of those people (Centaurs? Giants?). In the twenty-first century, some persons have applied a bias against those of Muslim faith to assert a broad assumption that all Muslims are security risks or even terrorists. Similar types of biases are demonstrated in the Potter series.

## BIAS AND THE TURNING OF KREACHER

It's particularly hard to work against a bias when the person in question is unlikeable. Think about the Black family's house-elf, Kreacher. His behavior is truly awful: He insults everyone constantly, he steals things from the house, he intentionally lets the house become dirty and gloomy, and he feeds information to the enemy when he can. He even contributes to the death of Sirius. But we have to wonder: If Sirius and the Order had had more respect for Kreacher's intelligence and experience—if they hadn't treated him as worthless and therefore powerless— could they have prevented him from causing so much harm?

In *Harry Potter and the Deathly Hallows,* Harry— after considering Hermione's psychological assessment of Kreacher—begins to treat the house-elf with respect and puts a Black family heirloom into his care. In return for this fair treatment, Kreacher gives Harry his loyalty, develops a less nasty attitude, and even joins Harry's side in the final battle against Voldemort! Whether you're a spy or a civilian, a Muggle or a wizard, how you treat others makes a huge difference in how they respond to you.

A lot of intelligence work starts with learning to think like your adversary. For example, during the Cold War era, veteran U.S. Air Force pilots learned to fly just as the pilots of the Soviet Union flew. Then, during so-called Red Flag exercises, new pilots practiced aerial combat by flying dogfights with these highly trained "Soviet" pilots. The U.S. Air Force was using the information it had gathered about the Soviet military practices to figure out how to train the U.S. "Red Team" pilots on how to perform just like Soviet pilots.

In *Harry Potter and the Half-Blood Prince*, Harry learns much about his adversary, Voldemort, in a very vivid way—by using the Pensieve to share others' memories of the young Tom Riddle as he developed his evil plans. Harry slowly discovers the terrifying facts about Voldemort's Horcruxes, but also useful information about how Voldemort's mind works: For example, Harry learns of Voldemort's bitterness and anger toward his

Muggle father and how it fuels his hatred of Muggles and half-breed wizards and witches. The psychological assessment that Harry builds from these many observations reveals to Harry Voldemort's strengths and weaknesses: Voldemort's hatred makes him ruthless, but also leaves him with no real friends. Many of his supporters serve him more out of fear than loyalty, and that makes them prone to desert him given the chance. And because Voldemort has no capacity to love—as Dumbledore so insightfully realized—he is unable to understand the true danger that Harry poses to him. Harry can't be defeated because he focuses on love, not hatred.

Voldemort employs his own psychological assessment of Harry as well. From it, he correctly guesses that Harry is desperate to have a family after years of neglect and abuse living with the Dursleys. That, plus Harry's habit of playing the hero, makes him vulnerable to Voldemort's implanted vision of Sirius being tortured by Voldemort himself.

A solid psychological assessment of a potential source or a sworn enemy can help intelligence officers to succeed. Knowing what motivates someone is a very powerful tool for a spy!

So, a good spy is someone who keeps a cool head, has a sharp eye for his or her surroundings, and knows how people work. In the next chapter, we'll look at how such a person might actually become a spy.

# CHAPTER 4

# ACTIVITIES

# Help the Bloody Baron

## Stumble upon the SLYTHERIN Common Room!

131

# 4·2. BREAKING THE CODE – DEFEATING DARK MAGIC

| | | |
|---|---|---|
| A – U | J – D | S – M |
| B – V | K – E | T – N |
| C – W | L – F | U – O |
| D – X | M – G | V – P |
| E – Y | N – H | W – Q |
| F – Z | O – I | X – R |
| G – A | P – J | Y – S |
| H – B | Q – K | Z – T |
| I – C | R – L | |

**1.** What was used to destroy *three* Horcruxes?

Z N K  Y C U X J  U L

MXELLOTJUX

**2.** What was used to destroy *two* of the other Horcruxes?

G  HGYOROYQ  LGTM

**3.** What destroyed the Ravenclaw Horcrux?

LOKTJLEXK

## 4.5. MATCHING - MATCH·MAKER, MATCH·MAKER - THE HOGWARTS DATING SCENE

List which boy is dating which girl (in chronological order) during the Harry Potter series.

The girls are: **Lavender Brown, Cho Chang, Penelope Clearwater, Hermione Granger, Madam Olympe Maxime, and Ginny Weasley**. And remember, some people dated more than one person!

Percy Weasley (*CS* 341). . . . . . . . . . . _____

Hagrid (*GF* 328) . . . . . . . . . . . . . . . _____

Viktor Krum (*GF* 414, 512). . . . . . . . _____

Cedric Diggory (*GF* 397, *OP* 231) . . . _____

Harry Potter (*OP* 457). . . . . . . . . . . . _____

Dean Thomas (*HBP* 121) . . . . . . . . . _____

Ron Weasley (*HBP* 300). . . . . . . . . . . _____

Harry Potter (*HBP* 533, *DH* 116). . . . _____

Ron Weasley (*DH* 625). . . . . . . . . . . . _____

## 4.4. MATCHING – SPY TERMS IN THE HARRY POTTER SERIES FOR SIXTH YEARS

Match the word with the term by putting the number of the term in the blank.

**21. handler**

_____ a group of people assigned to protect an important person—*Example*: Harry, when he is taken from the Dursleys' home at the beginning of each school term, often has one of these to protect and transport him.

**22. interrogation**

_____ a person stationed inside a government or spy agency who regularly provides information to another government or spy agency—*Example:* Unbeknownst to the "other" Prime Minister, his new assistant, Kingsley Shacklebolt, is actually working for the Ministry of Magic.

**23. mole**

_____ a lengthy questioning of a person, usually by an authority figure such as a police officer or detective—*Example:* At Harry's hearing, Cornelius Fudge asks Harry questions to get answers that Fudge wants to use against him.

**24. security detail**

_____ A senior intelligence officer in charge of an agent. *Example:* Dumbledore gave Snape assignments regarding his spying on Voldemort.

# 4.5. CROSSWORD - HARRY POTTER SPYCRAFT

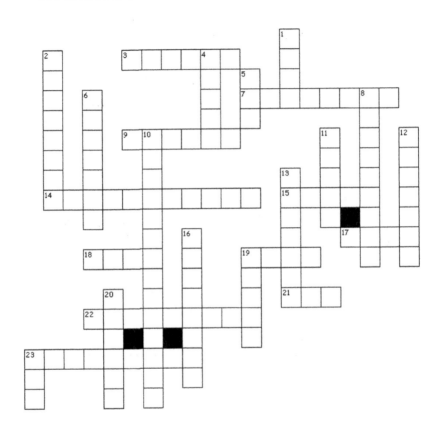

## ACROSS

3. An item or person that provides important information, including the Pensive

7. A type of message that uses regular words but hidden meaning understood by the reader, such as Harry's letter to "Snuffles" (2 words)

**9.** A detailed fake background about a person

**14.** Snape serves as this throughout the series, spying on Voldemort for Dumbledore (2 words)

**15.** The first name of Snape's handler

**17.** Kingsley Shacklebolt serves as one of these in his role of helping Britain's Prime Minister

**18.** The member of DA who as an intelligence analyst suggests that her team use thestrals to fly to the Ministry of Magic

**19.** A group of three or more people working covertly, such as Dumbledore's Army

**21.** The initials left at the end of the note found in the locket

**22.** Location where no one will find you, such as number twelve, Grimmauld Place, often used to debrief someone (2 words)

**23.** Hermione does this to get Rita Skeeter to write Harry's true story

## DOWN

**1.** 6 - 2 - 4 - 4 – 2 – which is one of these for "MAGIC"

**2.** A word or phrase that allows one entrance, such as what is given to the Pink Lady to get into Gryffindor Tower

**4.** A message or location that has any secret information removed

5. Riddle's first name

6. A person assigned to make sure the coast is clear, such as Ginny and Luna when Harry sneaks into Umbridge's office

8. Something caused, often by the Weasley twins, to distract someone

10. The Weasley twins use these to covertly listen (2 words)

11. Having confirmation that you weren't the one who did something wrong, like Harry having tea with Umbridge when the explosions went off

12. Someone or something, like Hedwig, that delivers messages

13. Dumbledore's role in assigning tasks to Snape

16. A written message or report intended for only one person's viewing (2 words)

19. False name or story

20. A person who unexpectedly arrives and offers his or her services as a covert agent, such as Snape when he agreed to spy for Dumbledore (2 words)

23. An electronic listening device, or Rita Skeeter

## 4·6. FILL IN THE BLANK – THE LIFE OF J. K. ROWLING (PUBLICATION YEARS) – PART 4

How well do you know Jo? Here is your chance to discover the details of her life and the sources of many of the Harry Potter characters. Just fill in the blank, if you can!

31. In 1994, Jo—writing completely in long-hand—completes *Harry Potter and the* _____ *Stone*, as it is named in England.

   **31. Answer:** _____

32. Jo can't afford to make photocopies of the book, so she types up two copies of the text on an old _____ to send to literary agents.

   **32. Answer:** _____

33. Jo receives a grant from the Scottish Arts Council, which allows her to pay for daycare while she works teaching _____.

   **33. Answer:** _____

34. Jo begins her new job exactly _____ year from when she previously stopped working and started writing full-time.

   **34. Answer:** _____

**35.** Jo finishes the storyline for the second book, _____ _of_
Secrets.

**35. Answer:** _____

**36.** After the first agent rejects her book, the second literary
agent, Christopher _____, agrees to represent Jo _Hint:_
_He plays a "big" part in Jo's life, even though his name is the_
_opposite._

**36. Answer:** _____

**37.** In 1996 a London publisher, _____, agrees to publish
the first Harry Potter book. _Hint: First half, a flower does_
_this when it is alive; second half, what you might do with_
_someone who is dead._

**37. Answer:** _____

**38.** Arthur Levine of _____ _____ wins the auction
for U.S. rights to the first book, paying $100,000. _Hint:_
_Every few months we would get the chance to order books in_
_school from this company._

**38. Answer:** _____ _____

**39.** _____ _Stone_ is published in England July 1997.

**39. Answer:** _____

**40.** _____ _Stone_ is published in the U.S. August 1998.

**40. Answer:** _____

## 4.7. FILL IN THE BLANK – MINISTRY OF MAGIC DIRECTORY – PART 1

### Level 1

"Level one, **1.**_____ of Magic and Support Staff" (*DH* 245).

*Hint: 1) Supposedly, he's in charge of the English Wizarding world.*

### Level 2

"Level two, Department of Magical Law **2.**_____, including the Improper **3.**_____ of Magic Office, **4.**_____ Headquarters, and Wizengamot Administration Services" (*OP* 130). Also Misuse of Muggle **5.**_____ (*OP* 132).

*Hint: Think 2) cops, 3) Harry saving Dudley and himself from the dementors, 4) Kingsley Shacklebolt, and 5) where Mr. Weasley works.*

### Level 3

"Level three, Department of Magical **6.**_____ and Catastrophes, including the Accidental **7.**_____ Reversal Squad, **8.**_____ Headquarters, and Muggle-Worthy Excuse Committee" (*OP* 130).

*Hint: Think 6) I didn't mean for it to happen, 7) 6 – 2 – 4 – 4- 2, 8) make that memory disappear!*

## 4·8. FILL IN THE BLANK – THE LIFE OF SEVERUS SNAPE (THE ASSIGNMENT) – PART 4

**22.** Snape does his best to save Dumbledore after the Headmaster's hand is wounded by the Horcrux _____ between Harry's _____ and _____ years (*DH* 680–83).

**22. Answers:** _____ _____ _____

**23.** Dumbledore is told by Snape that he has maybe _____ year to live; Snape promises to do all he can to protect the _____ if the school falls into Voldemort's grasp (*DH* 680–83).

**23. Answers:** _____ _____

**24.** Dumbledore then reveals that it is Snape who will have to kill _____, not Malfoy. Snape agrees to do so (*DH* 680–83).

**24. Answer:** _____

**25.** Snape objects to not being privy to all of Dumbledore's secrets; Dumbledore tells Snape that he cannot tell him everything because of the amount of time Snape spends with _____ —on Dumbledore's orders, Snape retorts (*DH* 683–84).

**25. Answer:** _____

**26.** Later that night Dumbledore tells Snape that a part of Voldemort's soul lives inside of _____ _____; because of this, he must die, and _____ is the one who must kill him (*DH* 686–87).

**26. Answer:** _____ _____, **and** _____

27. Snape keeps his promise and kills _____ in the presence of many witnesses (*HBP* 596).

**27. Answer:** _____

28. Dumbledore, through his portrait, instructs Snape to tell _____ the correct date of Harry's departure from the Weasley's home at the end of the summer, and to have someone suggest the use of other persons (who look just like Harry) as _____, and that Snape must act his part well if he is part of the attempt to capture Harry (*DH* 688).

**28. Answers:** _____ _____

# CHAPTER 4
# ANSWERS

# CHAPTER 4

## 4·1. ANSWERS TO MAZE – HELP THE BLOODY BARON FIND THE SLYTHERIN COMMON ROOM

# 4·2. ANSWERS TO BREAKING THE CODE – DEFEATING DARK MAGIC

1. The Sword of Gryffindor
2. A Basilisk Fang
3. Fiendfyre

In order of their destruction:

**1st** – Tom Riddle's Diary by **A Basilisk Fang**
**2nd** – Marvolo Gaunt's Ring by **The Sword of Gryffindor**
**3rd** – Salazar Slytherin's Locket by **The Sword of Gryffindor**
**4th** – Helga Hufflepuff's Cup by **A Basilisk Fang**
**5th** – Rowena Ravenclaw's Diadem by **Fiendfyre**
   [Harry by his "death"????]
**6th** – Nagini by **The Sword of Gryffindor**

# 4·3. ANSWERS TO MATCH·MAKER, MATCH·MAKER – THE HOGWARTS DATING SCENE:

Percy Weasley (*CS* 341) . . . . . . . . . . Penelope Clearwater
Hagrid (*GF* 328) . . . . . . . . . . . Madam Olympe Maxime
Viktor Krum (*GF* 414, 512). . . . . . . . . Hermione Granger
Cedric Diggory (*GF* 397, *OP* 231) . . . . . . . . . Cho Chang
Harry Potter (*OP* 457) . . . . . . . . . . . . . . . . . . Cho Chang
Dean Thomas (*HBP* 121) . . . . . . . . . . . . . Ginny Weasley
Ron Weasley (*HBP* 300) . . . . . . . . . . . . . Lavender Brown
Harry Potter (*HBP* 533, *DH* 116) . . . . . . . Ginny Weasley
Ron Weasley (*DH* 625) . . . . . . . . . . . . Hermione Granger

## 4.4. ANSWERS TO MATCHING – SPY TERMS IN THE HARRY POTTER SERIES FOR SIXTH YEARS

24 security detail, 23 mole, 22 interrogation, and 21 handler

## 4.5. ANSWERS TO CROSSWORD – HARRY POTTER SPYCRAFT

**Across**

3. SOURCE
7. OPEN CODE
9. LEGEND
14. DOUBLE AGENT
15. ALBUS
17. MOLE
18. LUNA
19. CELL
21. RAB
22. SAFE HOUSE
23. BLACKMAIL

**Down**

1. CODE
2. PASSWORD
4. CLEAN
5. TOM
6. LOOKOUT
8. DIVERSION
10. EXTENDABLE EARS
11. ALIBI
12. COURIER
13. HANDLER
16. EYES ONLY
19. COVER
20. WALK-IN
23. BUG

## 4·6. ANSWERS TO FILL IN THE BLANK – THE LIFE OF J. K. ROWLING (PUBLICATION YEARS) – PART 4

31. **Philosopher's**
32. **typewriter**
33. **French**
34. **one**
35. **Chamber**
36. **Little**
37. **Bloomsbury**
38. **Scholastic Press**
39. **Philosopher's**
40. **Sorcerer's**

## 4·7. ANSWERS TO FILL IN THE BLANK 7 – MINISTRY OF MAGIC DIRECTORY – PART 1

1. **Minister** of Magic and Support Staff
2. Department of Magical Law **Enforcement**
3. Improper **Use** of Magic Office
4. **Auror** Headquarters
5. Misuse of Muggle **Artifacts**
6. Department of Magical **Accidents** and Catastrophes
7. Accidental **Magic** Reversal Squad
8. **Obliviator** Headquarters

# 4·8. ANSWERS TO THE LIFE OF SEVERUS SNAPE (THE ASSIGNMENT) – PART 4

22. ring, 5th, 6th
23. one, students
24. him (Dumbledore)
25. Voldemort
26. Harry Potter, Voldemort
27. Dumbledore
28. Voldemort, decoys

# Chapter 5
## BECOMING A SPY

"AND YE SHALL KNOW THE TRUTH AND
THE TRUTH SHALL MAKE YOU FREE."

JOHN VIII—XXXII

CENTRAL INTELLIGENCE AGENCY

UNITED STATES OF AMERICA

So you're smart, you're dedicated, and you're observant. Like Harry Potter, you think quickly under pressure. Like Hermione, you soak up information and use it to seek out the truth. Like Dumbledore, you're a wise student of human nature. And you want to be a spy. What next?

## GETTING STARTED

It might seem strange, but to become a spy—or, at least, to be hired by an intelligence organization—you must be, first and foremost, a trustworthy person and upstanding citizen. Those who wish to become a spy with any organization that deals with secret information must have a history of reliability and high performance, including good grades in school and good references from teachers and employers.

Generally a college or university degree is the next important step. Most successful applicants for intelligence jobs get degrees in subjects such as political science, international relations, economics, law, foreign languages, math, or one of the sciences. They work hard and excel in these courses, and many take study-abroad courses or get involved in volunteer groups, campus publications, and other extracurricular activities. Finally, candidates for intelligence work should have no criminal record—for the most part they cannot have been convicted of a crime.

The careful selection of spies occurs in the Wizarding world as well. Aurors are highly trained spies or security agents who focus on application of Defense Against the Dark Arts, gathering information about those who are using the Dark

Arts and stopping them—in essence, combating Voldemort, Death Eaters, and others who use Dark Magic. They also serve as protectors of high-security assets: for example, Kingsley Shacklebolt is assigned at different times to protect Minister of Magic Cornelius Fudge, the Muggle Prime Minister, and of course Harry. Thus, Aurors are not only similar to case officers and intelligence analysts, but also fulfill the roles of FBI and Secret Service agents in the United States today, as well as the Royal Mounted Police of Canada.

Witches and wizards who wish to become Aurors must do very well in school, scoring an E (Exceeds Expectations) on at least five N.E.W.T.s (Nastily Exhausting Wizarding Tests). In *Harry Potter and the Order of the Phoenix,* Professor McGonagall explains that to become an Auror, Harry would need to "demonstrate the ability to react well to pressure and so forth," as well as "perseverance and dedication, because Auror training takes a further three years, not to mention very high skills in practical Defense" (p. 665).

Professor Umbridge then reminds Harry, rather unpleasantly, that he cannot become an Auror if he has been convicted of a crime. Dolores Umbridge is intentionally "forgetting" that Harry was cleared of all criminal charges for using the Patronus Charm against the Dementors that attacked him and Dudley in Little Whinging (because his use of magic was necessary for self-defense). But Professor Umbridge does have a point: conviction for even a minor crime could ruin Harry's chances for a career as an Auror. (If Harry had known that in his first years at school, perhaps he might have thought twice before going off on some of his more risky adventures!)

People who wish to work in the intelligence world,

especially those who wish to work as case officers, must also be healthy and physically fit. Eating a sensible diet and getting regular exercise is a good start. A strong athletic record is even better; a history of good performance and leadership in team sports can show that a candidate for an intelligence job works well with others and can commit to a goal, even in a lousy season. Harry's success with the Gryffindor Quidditch team, both as a star player and a successful captain, would definitely qualify as demonstrated commitment to a goal and good leadership skills.

It should come as no surprise that candidates for intelligence positions should not have a current drug or alcohol problem. Not only can substance abuse lead to career-ending criminal convictions, they can also make an intelligence officer a security risk. If an adversary observes an intelligence officer breaking the law by taking drugs or driving while drunk, for instance, that adversary has evidence that can be used to blackmail the intelligence officer and gain access to secret information. Intelligence officers are therefore required to inform their superiors of any such problems or mistakes—so the other side can't use it against them. A good spy never gives the other side the chance to take control.

## LANDING THE JOB

The next step toward becoming a spy is simple: apply to the agency of your choice, usually by sending a letter summarizing your essential personal qualifications, such as education, foreign travel, experience, languages, present occupation, and any special skills. Many people incorrectly assume that only the CIA uses spies and intelligence analysts, but in reality there are seventeen separate U.S. agencies that are responsible for providing intelligence. The information they gather is combined and delivered to the head U.S. intelligence officer, the Director of National Intelligence. These sixteen components under the Director of National Intelligence are shown below:

Director of National Intelligence

Air Force     Army     CIA     Coast Guard     DIA

Dept. of Energy     Homeland Security     Dept. of State     Dept. of Treasury     Dept. of Justice

FBI    Marines    Geospatial    NRO    NSA

Navy

Before applying anywhere, you should do some research. What are the principle functions and activities of the organization? Will you need to move to a new city to take the position? Are you willing to travel for your job, perhaps to dangerous places? Are you willing to work in a job that you can't discuss with your friends and family? And don't forget, the military services use military officers, enlisted personnel, *and civilians*; thus, you can be a civilian and still work for a branch of the military as an intelligence officer.

So, what do you do after selecting the agency or agencies that you would like to join? Fill out the online application form in which you provide all your background information as well as the contact information of the people who will give you good references, then just hit the button, and poof! You've started on your way to becoming a spy. (It goes without saying that you should be honest in all of your application materials. Who wants to hire a person who lies on day one?)

When Harry decides that he wants to become an Auror, he consciously begins observing the Aurors he knows as they work. He realizes that Kingsley Shacklebolt and Nymphadora Tonks—the Aurors who he knows best—work long hours in dangerous conditions. Harry rightfully observes that Mad-Eye Moody suffered permanent injuries on Auror assignments and is completely (and justifiably) paranoid about security even after his retirement as an Auror. Harry is well aware that many Aurors have died in the line of duty. The dangers are no different for modern-day spies.

In *Harry Potter and the Deathly Hallows*, Rufus Scrimgeour—prior Head of the Auror Office and now Minister of Magic—gruffly tries to convince Harry to cooperate with the Ministry of Magic, but Harry's loyalty is instead to Dumbledore and his friends in the Order of the Phoenix. Simply put, he doesn't trust the Ministry or Rufus Scrimgeour. (And, however ruthless Scrimgeour is in trying to convince Harry to side with the Ministry, it is important to note that he doesn't betray Harry when the Death Eaters torture and kill him.)

While you're doing your research on the organization, the agency does its own. It will compare your application against those of thousands of other people interested in the job. If you seem like a good candidate, the agency will contact you to get more information and to set up an interview. This is where it gets interesting!

Before an intelligence organization will offer you a position, you must first pass a background check, which is a thorough investigation of your life. The process begins when you fill out a detailed form describing everywhere you've lived, listing every job you've held, and naming all of your relatives and people who knew you at various times throughout your life. To find out whether you have been honest in your application and whether you would be a good candidate for the service, investigators interview the people you have listed and often other people named by those who were initially listed.

The investigators also look for anything that could be used against you as blackmail. They leave no stone unturned, for your history and background demonstrate a lot about your character, which is what the agency is really trying to evaluate.

Many agencies also do security clearance checks when someone already working for that organization requests a higher level of clearance. Additional security reviews may also occur whenever someone gets promoted or takes a new position. And if some negative fact comes to light, the agency will investigate to make sure that the person is still trustworthy and not vulnerable to turning.

Once you've passed your background check, the organization will set up additional interviews with the department interested in hiring you. This is a good time to ask questions based on your research. What kind of work will you be doing? Will you get training? How much are you expected to travel? Is there anything you can do to be better prepared for the position, if they hire you? What is the pay scale? Will you be undercover, and if so what can you tell others about your work? If the answer is nothing, what should you say instead of just nothing?

If you're one of the lucky few, you'll be offered a job!

## TRAINING

Once you accept the job, you will begin training in the skills and tools unique to the position you were hired to do. If you'll be working as an intelligence analyst, you'll learn to use the computer programs and archival systems that manage the organization's vast stores of data. If you're hired in a position that involves dangerous work, you will go through special training in weapons and defense. If you are hired to go into operational work, you will receive the training for tradecraft. If you are hired as an analyst, you will receive proper training in intelligence analysis.

If you speak one or more foreign languages, you may go through intense language courses that teach you vocabulary specific to the spy world, or that polish your skills to near-perfect fluency. Even the persons hired in other areas—such as scientists and engineers—receive special training that relates specifically to what the organization does and what that person will be doing.

Aurors in the Wizarding world also go through special training. In *Harry Potter and the Order of the Phoenix,* Tonks mentions taking a class in Concealment and Disguise, covering ways of changing one's appearance with wands, potions, and other such methods. Of course, as a Metamorphmagus, she only needs to *think* to change her appearance, so she understandably aced the class. However, Tonks did less well in the required Stealth and Tracking class—big surprise (given how clumsy she is)!

# THE FARM

The Farm is the CIA's training facility in Virginia, where case officers go through about six months of training (the exact location and length of training is classified). The course is tough—among other things, you have to spend a few days in a swamp trying to escape from people who are hunting you down! There is also a jail sequence, where you are put in jail, deprived of necessities, and interrogated.

Not all of the classes are that strenuous, though. You also learn how to conduct and avoid **surveillance**, gather information at parties, recruit agents, write reports, set up secret meetings, use communication gadgets, secretly open and reseal letters, pick locks, take photos without being caught, create disguises, drive defensively, handle a weapon, and much more.

*The Real Spy's Guide to Becoming a Spy* p. 83–84
Earnest with Harper (2009).

## SPYING: IN THE OFFICE AND IN THE FIELD

Like most professionals, spies are never done with training—they keep learning all the time, from experience as well as continuing classes and training exercises. But after a few intense weeks of training, new intelligence professionals get down to business.

Possibly the most important part of working in the spy world is learning to work with a team. Throughout the Potter books the members of the Order of the Phoenix (as well as Dumbledore's Army) work together, share assignments, and often literally fight for each other. They work as a team. They share the risks and always have each other's back. This is especially true when Ron, Hermione, Neville, Luna, and Ginny insist on assisting Harry in rescuing Sirius from the Department of Mysteries.

When new case officers take their first assignment, the first step involves the efforts of many intelligence professionals working together, usually at the organization's headquarters. Experts on the target location (usually a foreign country or a particular business) create a cover story for the case officer. The case officer is briefed on what she or he might face on the ground: the local political situation, cultural customs, social tensions, even the clothes people are expected to wear. This is called "reading in"—that is, reading the files, receiving the briefings, and learning all you need to know to do the mission. If the posting requires foreign-language experience, an expert in that language might help the case officer brush up on his or her language skills.

# CHAPTER 5

# SENIOR INTELLIGENCE OFFICERS

When an intelligence officer has worked for many years in an organization, possibly in many different areas, and completed many successful missions, he or she may be promoted to a management position directing other case officers. These senior case officers have experience in how the various branches of intelligence work and how to get the desired information. Most of these senior intelligence officers have experience in field work (as well as analysis) and know what it's like to take direction in the field.

A senior case officer at the location you have been assigned (usually the CIA chief of station) is in charge of the overall mission of the station and coordinates the details relating to various operations. This is the person who will oversee preparations for the mission, keep tabs on everyone involved as the mission takes place, and ensure that the case officer has everything needed to get the job done.

When the case officer delivers information back to the senior case officer, he or she works with intelligence analysts and others to evaluate the information, compare it to other sources of intelligence, and put everything together in a report sent to headquarters.

The senior intelligence officer's job is not an easy one. At his or her direction, loyal and dedicated people undertake dangerous work—and some spies do die in the line of duty. Even people who never go undercover or carry a gun can be hurt while working in the intelligence field. Being unable to talk about your job to anyone is isolating, and the emotional toll can ruin friendships and cause turmoil within families. A good intelligence officer must be aware of how the stress of espionage work affects the members of his or her team. And even an accomplished spy can make mistakes.

The true master spy of the world of Harry Potter is Professor Dumbledore. He has decades of practice in psychological analysis. He has hunted down some of the best-hidden secrets in the Wizarding world. Most of all, he maintains his equanimity in the most desperate moments, and he keeps secrets well—perhaps all too well. His understanding of Snape's motivations allows him to "turn" one of Voldemort's closest allies, creating a true double agent that serves him loyally for many years. And Dumbledore's understanding of Voldemort, partially through Snape, provides the key to defeating the Dark Lord.

## EVERYONE IS PART OF THE TEAM

The world of Muggle espionage needs many people to keep it running. Many of these jobs are not what you'd think of as exciting. But the analyst who combs through every word in every newspaper and blog post from an important city might turn up the clue that gets an undercover person out safely. The security guard who spends hours guarding a single door might notice the telltale signs that someone has tried to break into a secure facility—before secrets can be stolen. And the undercover person who shows up to the same boring office job every day might be in just the right place to overhear the secret that, combined with other intelligence, saves lives down the road. And, of course, there's always the covert agent, dressed to the nines, who crashes a party, sneaks into the target's office, cracks the safe, and photographs the adversary's secret plans. None of them can work effectively without the support of all the others. Together, they seek the truth, however deeply buried it might be.

## PLANNING A MISSION: *OPERATION FIREPLACE*

OPERATION:
UMBRIDGE OFFICE
1. existing security
2. risk analysis
3. layout
4. inside risks
5. communication plan
6. time constraints
7. don't leave a trace
8. getting out
9. calling BINGO

The missions that Harry undertakes involve substantial preparation and planning. *Harry Potter and the Order of the Phoenix* has an excellent example of ops planning: Harry's mission is to break into Professor Umbridge's office so he can talk to Sirius. At this point in the story, Harry has discovered a lot of new information, some of it unsettling, and he needs to talk to Sirius Black in order to sort it out. However, Professor Umbridge, in her campaign to force Hogwarts to follow the Ministry of Magic's rules, is intercepting students' mail, restricting student communications, and spying on the Floo network. Harry is aware that there is only one place where he can communicate with Sirius without being detected, and that is from Professor Umbridge's own fireplace in her office. If she catches Harry talking to Sirius, he'll be thrown out of school, and Sirius's cover will be blown. Thus, Harry's mission is to contact Sirius, who is presently at the Order's headquarters, without the knowledge of his enemies.

## THE PLAN

With this goal in mind, let's walk through our friends' operations planning process for this mission. As in any plan, it is essential that everyone knows what they are supposed to do, when they are going to do it, and how long they have to complete their tasks. In the Muggle world, this often starts with an intelligence briefing, in which an intelligence officer updates the operations team on what the organization knows about the target location, the individuals who could be there, and other details important to the mission. (Such information is often stored in a SCIF.) Harry's operation includes similar planning.

The students already have much of the information that an intelligence briefing would include and have already decided to have the Weasley twins create a distraction (diversion) to get Professor Umbridge out of her office. Let's review what mission planning questions our friends discuss (or should have) discussed) in getting ready for *Operation Fireplace*.

1. *What is the security used to prevent access?* The door to Umbridge's office is protected with a bespelled lock. They plan to open it with the penknife that Sirius gave Harry as a Christmas gift. It will open any lock and undo any knot, even magical ones.

2. *What are the risks associated with getting into the location?* Umbridge will be suspicious of the distraction and will jump on any excuse to expel Harry, so the most obvious risk is being observed in the hallway. Harry will use the Invisibility Cloak to

avoid being observed, in addition to relying on the twins' diversion to draw everyone away from the office.

3. *What is the layout of the area around the location and inside the location itself?* The students know the layout of the corridors near the office because they pass by it regularly during the school day. Harry also knows the layout of the office all too well from his detentions in Umbridge's office.

4. *What are the risks relating to being observed while inside the location?* In other words, are there any cameras or other devices (such as a Sneakoscope) that could observe Harry when he enters and alert Umbridge? Will there be any security alerts or magic spells that go off when someone is in the office? Harry does not think this is an issue because he has not observed Umbridge turning off any mechanisms when entering the room or arming alarms when leaving it.

5. *How is the communication device (the fireplace) activated?* Harry will use Floo powder to activate the network and contact Sirius. Here's a point where the ops team makes a potential mistake: they should ask themselves, where will Harry get the Floo powder? A well-planned operation provides the case officer with everything needed—including the means of initiating communication. Part of the plan should have included Harry bringing his own supply of Floo

powder with him. Lucky for Harry, there is Floo powder sitting on the hearth that he is able to use.

6. *What are the time constraints? How long can the operation last?* Nobody knows how long the twins' distraction will keep Umbridge busy. The Weasley twins estimate that their diversion will keep Umbridge busy for at least twenty minutes. When the timing is this uncertain, the answer should be "get in and out as fast as possible." This is another weakness in the plan: Harry should think about how long it will take to get into the office and activate the network, how long it will take for Sirius to answer his call, and how much time he will need to get information from his godfather.

At the very least, he should have taken a stopwatch or other timer to alert him when his time is up. (You may recall that the second time Harry breaks into Umbridge's office to see if Sirius is at headquarters and not being tortured by Voldemort at the Department of Mysteries, he loses track of time and gets caught because of it.)

7. *What must be done to leave the location exactly the same?* Harry must leave no trace of the break-in, or else Umbridge will know that someone has used her fireplace and some kind of message got out. The whole point of a covert operation is to go in, do what you need to do, and get out—all without anybody knowing you were there! First, will the door show

any sign of forced entry? Harry knows that the knife doesn't leave any marks on the locks it opens. He can't be sure, however, whether it leaves a magical trail—something to research ahead of time, don't you think?

Once inside, he should be careful not to knock anything over or leave marks on any dusty shelves. After he uses the Floo powder, he must put the container back in exactly the same place it was when he arrived. (Even better, he should bring his own Floo powder, so that Umbridge doesn't notice that there's less left in the box than she remembers.) And when he finishes his chat, he should tidy up the fireplace so that there's no evidence that he used it.

In the Muggle world, case officers often use a digital camera to photograph a location as they enter it. (If the room must remain dark, they use low-light equipment.) Before they leave, they can compare the first photo with how the room looks just before they leave and make sure that everything matches.

## BLACK BAG JOBS—COVERT OPERATIONS AT THEIR BEST

A **black bag job** involves breaking into a home, office, or other location without the knowledge of the owner. The term comes from the black bag full of tools needed to get inside, such as lock-picking tools, ropes, or drills. A black bag job is a success when the case officer gets inside, obtains the secret information (or conceals bugs or other surveillance devices), and leaves undetected and without the knowledge of the person who works or lives there.

~~~~~~~~~~~~~~~~~~~~~~~~~~~~~~~~~~~~~~~

8. *Once the mission is complete, how will the team leave without being seen?* Harry plans to leave under the Invisibility Cloak. But will he simply open the door, step out, and walk away? What if there's someone in the hall outside, or someone comes into the office while he is in there? Will there be lookouts? A good ops planner thinks through all of the details, far beyond the moment when the goal is achieved!

9. *Is there a way for the team to communicate if they need to call off the mission?* It is essential in any plan to have a way to communicate if something goes wrong. Harry needs to know right away if Umbridge isn't where she's supposed to be, or if she's on her way back—but he has not planned for this. There should be a lookout. The ability to call off a plan is very important for keeping everyone involved in the mission safe and reducing risk. It's never too early to think of ways to stop the mission while in progress.

## THE MISSION

Now that the plan is in place, it's time to execute. Will our friends' preparations hold up, or will they fall apart in the face of unpredictable reality?

The first part of the mission goes well. The twins set off their distraction, and Professor Umbridge races off to deal with it. Harry slips into the Invisibility Cloak, uses the knife to get into the office, and activates the Floo network. (He waits to take the Cloak off when he gets inside the office, properly remaining invisible as long as possible!)

Harry uses the box of Floo powder next to the fireplace to activate the network and announces the address of the fireplace he wants to connect with: number twelve, Grimmauld Place. This is a huge risk: if there is a bug recording sounds in the office or some magical method for Umbridge to hear what is happening in her office, Harry has just given away the secret address of the Order's headquarters! Lucky for him, Umbridge does not have such security devices in place.

Harry first talks to Lupin, who calls Sirius to the fire—taking up precious time. They talk about the issues that have been weighing on Harry's mind: the bad behavior of his father at Hogwarts and the reasons behind Snape's hatred. Harry loses track of time; lucky for him, there is a pause in the conversation just as footsteps sound outside the office door. Because Harry did not post a lookout, he barely has time to hide himself under the invisibility cloak before Filch enters the office to retrieve some papers. After Filch leaves Harry makes sure the invisibility cloak is completely covering him and exits the office.

Through *Operation Fireplace* Harry is now in possession of some new information: his father's bad behavior at school was not a lie concocted by Snape, but his godfather's acceptance of it doesn't line up with Harry's personal belief in what is right. None of these facts provides an instant solution to Harry's problems, but it does give him useful material for psychological analysis of Lupin and Sirius, as well as a better understanding of Snape's motivations.

Once a mission is over the participants should meet and reflect on how the mission went and analyze what could be done differently, as well as evaluate the costs of the mission with the gains. In both the military and the intelligence world this is called the debrief. So what can we say about the mission afterwards? From Harry's standpoint, he now has more information, but some of it is disturbing. He has confirmed that his father behaved badly in regards to Snape. Moreover, he has lost some confidence in the rightness of his godfather's motivations—a hard thing to accept. Plus, after the chaos and mess caused by their distraction, the Weasley twins decide to leave Hogwarts before Umbridge can throw them out.

Thus Harry's mission has succeeded, but two members of his team—two good friends—have left Hogwarts as a result of participation in *Operation Fireplace*. Finally, Umbridge is likely to crack down even harder on students after the Weasleys' diversion and colorful exit, along with the creation of the Portable Swamp, making life even harder for Harry and his friends. A successful mission is worth celebrating, but one must always take into account not only what was gained, but what was lost.

## THE ETHICS OF SPYING—KNOWING THE DIFFERENCE BETWEEN RIGHT AND WRONG

In every Harry Potter book, the characters always find themselves challenged to behave ethically. Ethics is really nothing more than deciding what is right and wrong and acting on it. Friendship, love, loyalty, and empathy win out over greed, thoughtless ambition, and deceit, though often at great cost. But what is right and wrong isn't as clear in the spy world. Intelligence organizations train their case officers to lie and deceive, and they use other people to get what they want, sometimes, though rarely, through threats and blackmail. Spies are often asked to break the laws of foreign countries even while obeying the laws of their own country to the letter. However, the secrets gained can be used to protect millions of U.S. citizens and billions of innocent people worldwide. Anyone who wants to become a spy should think hard about what they are willing to do to serve and protect his or her country. The demands are high, often for work that no one can ever know you did.

## AND THE TRUTH SHALL MAKE YOU FREE

Visitors to the lobby of the Central Intelligence Agency building see chiseled into the marble wall the motto of the CIA. The motto is a verse from the Bible, John 8:32: "And ye shall know the truth and the truth shall make you free." That means getting to the real truth of the matter (or at least as close as possible), even if your own side has gotten it wrong. One of the best skills taught in spy training is the ability to question everything and look at all sides of a situation, even if it means doubting your own organization. Speaking truth to power is the fundamental duty of the CIA and all of the other intelligence agencies.

# CHAPTER 5

# ACTIVITIES

# 5.1. BREAKING THE CODE – PASSWORDS TO GET INTO GRYFFINDOR TOWER

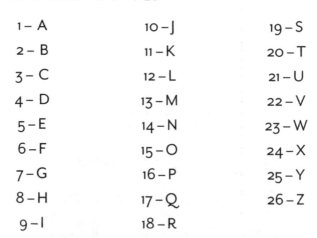

| | | |
|---|---|---|
| 1 – A | 10 – J | 19 – S |
| 2 – B | 11 – K | 20 – T |
| 3 – C | 12 – L | 21 – U |
| 4 – D | 13 – M | 22 – V |
| 5 – E | 14 – N | 23 – W |
| 6 – F | 15 – O | 24 – X |
| 7 – G | 16 – P | 25 – Y |
| 8 – H | 17 – Q | 26 – Z |
| 9 – I | 18 – R | |

**Password 1 –** At the very end of the corridor hung a portrait of a very fat woman in a pink silk dress. "Password?" she said.

"_____ _____," said Percy (*SS* 129).

3  1  16  21  20   4  18  1  3  15  14  9  19

**Password 2 –** "The password's '_____ _____' but it won't help you now, the Fat Lady's gone off somewhere" (*SS* 156).

16  9  7   19  14  15  21  20

**Password 3 –** "It's '_____,'" said Hermione (*CS* 84).

23 1 20 20 12 5 2 9 18 4

| | | | | | | | | | |
|---|---|---|---|---|---|---|---|---|---|
| | | | | | | | | | |

**Password 4 –** "The new password's '_____ _____'!" (*PA* 94, 152)

6 15 18 20 21 14 1    13 1 10 15 18

| | | | | | | |
|---|---|---|---|---|---|---|
| | | | | | | |

| | | | | |
|---|---|---|---|---|
| | | | | |

**Password 5 –** "_____ _____," said Ron (*PA* 230).

19 3 21 18 22 25    3 21 18

| | | | | | |
|---|---|---|---|---|---|
| | | | | | |

| | | |
|---|---|---|
| | | |

**Password 6 –** "_____," said Harry to Sir Cadogan (*PA* 249).

15 4 4 19 2 15 4 9 11 9 14 19

| | | | | | | | | | | | |
|---|---|---|---|---|---|---|---|---|---|---|---|
| | | | | | | | | | | | |

**Password 7 –** They passed the security trolls, gave the Fat Lady the password (" _____ ") (*PA* 295).

6 12 9 2 2 5 18 20 9 7 9 2 2 5 20

| | | | | | | | | | | | | | | |
|---|---|---|---|---|---|---|---|---|---|---|---|---|---|---|
| | | | | | | | | | | | | | | |

| 1 – A | 10 – J | 19 – S |
|-------|--------|--------|
| 2 – B | 11 – K | 20 – T |
| 3 – C | 12 – L | 21 – U |
| 4 – D | 13 – M | 22 – V |
| 5 – E | 14 – N | 23 – W |
| 6 – F | 15 – O | 24 – X |
| 7 – G | 16 – P | 25 – Y |
| 8 – H | 17 – Q | 26 – Z |
| 9 – I | 18 – R | |

**Password 8** – "_____," said George (*GF* 191).

2   1   12   4   5   18   4   1   19   8

| | | | | | | | | | |
|--|--|--|--|--|--|--|--|--|--|
| | | | | | | | | | |

**Password 9** – "_____ _____," he said dully to the Fat Lady (*GF* 398).

6   1   9   18   25          12   9   7   8   20   19

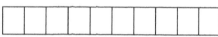

**Password 10** – This time it was Ron who waited outside to give the Fat Lady the password ("_____ _____") (*GF* 459).

2   1   14   1   14   1          6   18   9   20   20   5   18   19

| | | | | | |
|--|--|--|--|--|--|
| | | | | | |

**Password 11 –** He waved the stunted little cactus he had shown them on the train. "_____ _____!" (*OP* 216)

13  9  13  2  21  12  21  19

| | | | | | | | |
|---|---|---|---|---|---|---|---|

13  9  13  2  12  5  20  15  14  9  1

| | | | | | | | | | | |
|---|---|---|---|---|---|---|---|---|---|---|

**Password 12 –** "_____," said Harry to the Fat Lady (*HBP* 308).

2  1  21  2  12  5  19

| | | | | | | |
|---|---|---|---|---|---|---|

**Password 13 –** "Oh, hang on—password. _____" (*HBP* 351).

1  2  19  20  9  14  5  14  3  5

| | | | | | | | | | |
|---|---|---|---|---|---|---|---|---|---|

**Password 14 –** "The password's still '_____'!" (*HBP* 493)

20  1  16  5  23  15  18  13

| | | | | | | | |
|---|---|---|---|---|---|---|---|

# 5·2. MATCHING – SPY TERMS IN THE HARRY POTTER SERIES FOR SEVENTH YEARS

Match the word with the term by putting the number of the term in the blank.

**25. countermeasures**

_____ An agent left for an extended period, sometimes even years, awaiting a particular assignment or a signal indicating that the time has come to execute a preplanned mission. *Example:* Mrs. Figg is a sleeper agent assigned by Dumbledore to watch over Harry and act only if the circumstances warrant it, such as when she intercedes after Harry and Dudley are attacked by Dementors.

**26. eyes-only communication**

_____ Acts or devices that prevent someone from observing a spy's activities. *Example:* In order to prevent the children from listening in on the Order of the Phoenix's meetings with Extendable Ears, Mrs. Weasley employs countermeasures (an Imperturbable Charm) on the door.

**27. sleeper agent**

_____ Information that is so important that it can only be shown to the recipient— usually the leader of a country—and not left in that person's possession in the form of a paper or electronic copy. *Example:* Dumbledore shows Harry the memories he has collected in the Pensieve; the memories have not been transcribed or copied, making them more secure.

## 5.3. FILL IN THE BLANK – THE LIFE OF J. K. ROWLING (THE MOVIE YEARS) – PART 5

How well do you know Jo? Here is your chance to discover the details of her life and the sources of many of the Harry Potter characters. Just fill in the blank, if you can!

**41.** Warner Bros. obtains movie rights to *Sorcerer's Stone*, planning on using _____ _____ as the director. *Hint:* E.T., Jaws, Raiders of the Lost Ark, Bridge of Spies.

**41. Answer:** _____ _____

**42.** The planned director bows out of the project, so _____ _____ is hired to direct the first movie. *Hint: Perhaps he sailed the ocean blue . . . had he lived in 1492.*

**42. Answer:** _____ _____

**43.** In June 2000, Jo receives her first honorary degree from _____. *Hint: It is a private Ivy League school in Hanover, New Hampshire.*

**43. Answer:** _____

**44.** In 2001, Jo receives The Order of the British Empire (O.B.E.) from the royal family, specifically from His Royal Highness the Prince of _____, for services to children's literature.

**44. Answer:** _____

**45.** In early 2001, Jo is introduced to Dr. Neil Murray, an anesthesiologist, who at that point had only read the first

_____ pages of Jo's first book—which Jo considers a plus (he doesn't know much about it). *Hint: deca*

**45. Answer:** _____

46. Jo and Neil plan a quiet wedding at the _____ Islands, but the press finds out and the wedding is postponed. *Hint: Darwin was unable to attend, though he most certainly made it famous.*

**46. Answer:** _____

47. As a _____ present to themselves, Jo and Neil are married on December 26, 2001.

**47. Answer:** _____

48. Jo hints that someone important will _____ in the next book, *Order of the Phoenix*, which is finished by Jo in December 2002.

**48. Answer:** _____

49. _____ Gordon Rowling Murray is born on March 24, 2003, and _____ Jean Rowling Murray is born January 23, 2005. *Hint: Goliath and northern Scottish clan*

**49. Answers:** _____ **and** _____

50. On June 5, 2008, Jo delivers the commencement address at Harvard University entitled, "The Fringe Benefits of _____, and the Importance of Imagination." *Hint: She didn't talk about success, that's for sure.*

**50. Answer:** _____

## 5.4. FILL IN THE BLANK – MINISTRY OF MAGIC DIRECTORY – PART 2

### Level 4
"Level four, Department for the Regulation and Control of Magical **9.**_____, incorporating Beast, Being, and Spirit Divisions, **10.**_____ Liaison Office, and Pest Advisory Bureau" (*OP* 130).

*Hint: 9) homonym of the Black family house-elf; 10) they run the Wizarding bank.*

### Level 5
"Level five, Department of **11.**_____ Magical Cooperation, incorporating the International Magical Trading Standards Body, the International Magical Office of Law, and the International Confederation of Wizards, British Seats" (*OP* 130).

*Hint: 11) all of the subdivisions listed include reference to it.*

### Level 6
"Level six, Department of Magical Transport, incorporating the **12.**_____ Network Authority, **13.**_____ Regulatory Control, **14.**_____ Office, and **15.**_____ Test Center" (*OP* 129).

*Hint: think 12) fireplace, 13) need it to play Quidditch, 14) touch it, and you are someplace else, 15) whatever you do, don't Splinch yourself when doing it for the first time!*

## 5.5. FILL IN THE BLANK – THE LIFE OF SEVERUS SNAPE (THE FINAL SACRIFICE) – PART 5

**29.** Snape Confunds _____ _____ to suggest using decoys (*DH* 688).

**29. Answer:** _____ _____

**30.** During the chase after the decoys, Snape tries to hit the arm of a Death Eater who is aiming at Lupin's back, but misses, hitting _____ _____ instead (*DH* 74), who later claims to Fred he is now "holy" as a result.

**30. Answer:** _____ _____

**31.** Once headquarters has been compromised, Snape searches _____ _____'s old room at Grimmauld Place and finds the picture of _____ _____ and a letter signed by her; he keeps the two items, after tearing the picture and keeping her image only (*DH* 688–89).

**31. Answers:** _____ _____ **and**

_____ _____

**32.** Snape is then appointed _____ of Hogwarts (*DH* 227).

**32. Answer:** _____

**33.** Using his doe Patronus, Snape gets _____ _____ _____ _____ (four words) to Harry, using his Patronus to lure Harry to the lake where Snape has previously placed the item (*DH* 365–66, 367–70, 689).

**33. Answer:** _____ _____ _____ _____

**34.** During the battle of Hogwarts, Snape repeatedly asks Voldemort to let him find _____ _____ himself, but Voldemort refuses his request (*DH* 652, 654, 655).

**34. Answer:** _____ _____

**35.** Snape is attacked by Voldemort's snake, _____; Voldemort takes Snape's wand in the process, thinking it is the _____ Wand; Voldemort leaves, but before Snape dies he gives Harry his _____ (*DH* 656–58).

**35. Answer:** _____, _____, _____

# CHAPTER 5

# ANSWERS

# 5·1. ANSWERS TO BREAKING THE CODE S – PASSWORDS TO GET INTO GRYFFINDOR TOWER:

**Password 1** – **Caput Draconis** (*SS* 129)
**Password 2** – **Pig snout** (*SS* 156)
**Password 3** – **Wattlebird** (*CS* 84)
**Password 4** – **Fortuna Major** (*PA* 94, 152)
**Password 5** – **Scurvy cur** (*PA* 230)
**Password 6** – **Oddsbodikins** (*PA* 249)
**Password 7** – **Flibbertigibbet** (*PA* 295)
**Password 8** – **Balderdash** (*GF* 191)
**Password 9** – **Fairy lights** (*GF* 398)
**Password 10** – **Banana fritters** (*GF* 459)
**Password 11** – **Mimbulus mimbletonia** (*OP* 216)
**Password 12** – **Baubles** (*HBP* 308)
**Password 13** – **Abstinence** (*HBP* 351)
**Password 14** – **Tapeworm** (*HBP* 493)

# 5·2. ANSWERS TO MATCHING – SPY TERMS IN THE HARRY POTTER SERIES FOR SEVENTH YEARS

**27 sleeper agent, 25 countermeasures, and 26 eyes-only communication**

# 5.3. ANSWERS TO FILL IN THE BLANK – THE LIFE OF J. K. ROWLING (THE MOVIE YEARS) – PART 5

41. **Steven Spielberg**
42. **Chris Columbus**
43. **Dartmouth**
44. **Wales**
45. **ten**
46. **Galápagos**
47. **Christmas**
48. **die**
49. **David** and **Mackenzie**
50. **Failure**

# 5.4. ANSWERS TO FILL IN THE BLANK – MINISTRY OF MAGIC DIRECTORY – PART 2

9. Department for the Regulation and Control of Magical **Creatures**
10. **Goblin** Liaison Office, and Pest Advisory Bureau
11. Department of **International** Magical Cooperation
12. **Floo** Network Authority
13. **Broom** Regulatory Control
14. **Portkey** Office
15. **Apparation** Test Center

# 5.5. ANSWERS TO THE LIFE OF SEVERUS SNAPE (THE FINAL SACRIFICE) – PART 5

29. Mundungus Fletcher
30. George Weasley
31. Sirius Black's, Lily Potter (now married)
32. Headmaster
33. The Sword of Gryffindor
34. Harry Potter
35. Nagini, Elder, memories

# Chapter 6
## CONCLUSION

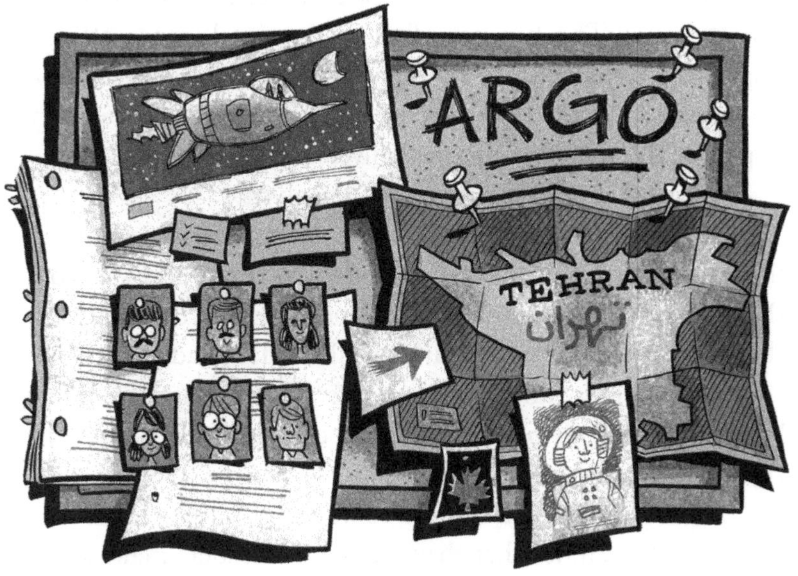

ARGO
TEHRAN
تهران

# CHAPTER 6

In the 2012 film *Argo,* a CIA intelligence officer travels to Iran in 1980, shortly after militants take over the American embassy there. The spy's mission is to rescue six U.S. State Department employees who had been working at the embassy but managed to escape capture when the embassy had been taken over by the Iranians. The intelligence officer and the six employees escape Iran by posing as a scouting crew for a science-fiction film.

This is all true, although there were really two CIA officers involved in the plan, one a case officer and the other an expert forger. The heroism of those two intelligence officers might have remained a secret forever had not President Clinton authorized CIA Director George Tenet to declassify the story as part of the agency's fiftieth-anniversary celebrations.

We need spies. And really good analysts.

Severus Snape is perhaps the best spy ever portrayed in literature. But we must remember that there are real spies out there, spies who take many risks, some dying in the process, their stars etched into the marble wall at CIA headquarters.

The world is full of risk. It is a very dangerous place. Only by having access to good information can our leaders make the right decisions.

And information is hard to come by.

Countries hide what they are doing. Leaders make statements that are intentionally false. And informants volunteer information that is often untrustworthy or just plain wrong.

It is intelligence professionals who seek the truth from a blurry world.

Leaders cannot make decisions without reliable information. The role of an intelligence service is not only to provide educated estimates, but also to synthesize known facts.

# CONCLUSION

In a democracy or representative government, intelligence services are used to protect its people from threats, understand and act against its adversaries, and further democratic ideals. The function of an intelligence agency in a free society is *to speak truth to power.* However, in non-democratic governments, often law enforcement and intelligence services, along with the military, are the primary instruments used to repress their own people. They are not concerned with truth, but power.

In the Muggle world, most spies in the field gather information through various sources—recruiting foreign citizens, reviewing open source materials, and observing, ever so carefully, what is going on around them. Yes, there are spies who pick locks, romance persons with access to get information, and shoot bad guys like the famous 007. But most spies look just like normal people, working quietly, surrounded by danger—waiting for opportunities to observe something important. These people relay information back home without a single explosion or shot fired.

Back home, there are thousands of intelligence professionals who organize and analyze every bit of that information. From it, they create reports that are read at the very highest levels of government.

Some spies sit at desks as analysts; others delve into the world as case officers. But both are necessary, and the world needs more of both types of spies.

The best and the brightest serve our country as case officers, intelligence officers, and intelligence analysts.

And by the way: Spying is fun.
They just can't talk about it.

# CHAPTER 6
# ACTIVITIES

# 6·1. BREAKING THE CODE – PASSWORDS TO GET INTO HEADMASTER'S TOWER

| | | |
|---|---|---|
| 1 – A | 10 – J | 19 – S |
| 2 – B | 11 – K | 20 – T |
| 3 – C | 12 – L | 21 – U |
| 4 – D | 13 – M | 22 – V |
| 5 – E | 14 – N | 23 – W |
| 6 – F | 15 – O | 24 – X |
| 7 – G | 16 – P | 25 – Y |
| 8 – H | 17 – Q | 26 – Z |
| 9 – I | 18 – R | |

**Password 15** – "_____ _____!" she said (*CS* 204).

| 12 | 5 | 13 | 15 | 14 | | 4 | 18 | 15 | 16 |
|---|---|---|---|---|---|---|---|---|---|

**Password 16** – "Sugar Quill! _____ _____!" (*GF* 579)

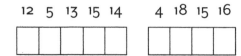

| 3 | 15 | 3 | 11 | 18 | 15 | 1 | 3 | 8 | | 3 | 12 | 21 | 19 | 20 | 5 | 18 |
|---|---|---|---|---|---|---|---|---|---|---|---|---|---|---|---|---|

**Password 17** – P.S. I enjoy _____ _____ (*HBP* 181, 196).

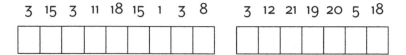

| 1 | 3 | 9 | 4 | | 16 | 15 | 16 | 19 |
|---|---|---|---|---|---|---|---|---|

**Password 18 – "_____ _____"** to Dumbledore's gargoyle, (*HBP* 493).

20 15 6 6 5 5      5 3 12 1 9 18 19

| | | | | | | |
|-|-|-|-|-|-|-|

| | | | | | | | |
|-|-|-|-|-|-|-|-|

**Password 19 – "Password?" "_____!"** said Harry (*DH* 662).

4 21 13 2 12 5 4 15 18 5

| | | | | | | | | | |
|-|-|-|-|-|-|-|-|-|-|

# 6·2. BREAKING THE CODE – PASSWORDS FOR OTHER PLACES OR POTTERWATCH

| | | |
|---|---|---|
| 1 – A | 10 – J | 19 – S |
| 2 – B | 11 – K | 20 – T |
| 3 – C | 12 – L | 21 – U |
| 4 – D | 13 – M | 22 – V |
| 5 – E | 14 – N | 23 – W |
| 6 – F | 15 – O | 24 – X |
| 7 – G | 16 – P | 25 – Y |
| 8 – H | 17 – Q | 26 – Z |
| 9 – I | 18 – R | |

**Passwords to Get Into Slytherin Tower:**

**Password 20** – "Oh, yeah—_____-_____!" said Malfoy (*CS* 221).

16 21 18 5 - 2 12 15 15 4

**Passwords to Get Into Prefects' Bathroom**

**Password 21** – "Password's '_____ _____'" (*GF* 431, 459).

16 9 14 5    6 18 5 19 8

| 1 – A | 10 – J | 19 – S |
|-------|--------|--------|
| 2 – B | 11 – K | 20 – T |
| 3 – C | 12 – L | 21 – U |
| 4 – D | 13 – M | 22 – V |
| 5 – E | 14 – N | 23 – W |
| 6 – F | 15 – O | 24 – X |
| 7 – G | 16 – P | 25 – Y |
| 8 – H | 17 – Q | 26 – Z |
| 9 – I | 18 – R | |

**Passwords to Listen to Potterwatch:**

**Password 22** – "I've got it, I've got it! Password was '_____'!" (*DH* 438)

1  12  2  21  19

|   |   |   |   |   |
|---|---|---|---|---|
|   |   |   |   |   |

**Password 23** – "The next password will be '_____-_____'" (*DH* 444).

13  1  4  -  5  25  5

|   |   |   | - |   |   |   |
|---|---|---|---|---|---|---|
|   |   |   | - |   |   |   |

# 6·3. MATCHING – SPY TERMS IN THE HARRY POTTER SERIES FOR HOGWARTS ALUMNAE

Match the word with the term by putting the number of the term in the blank.

**28. all-source intelligence**

_____ The person or entity receiving intelligence information, such as a head of state or other senior official with decision-making authority. *Example:* Harry Potter, as the person destined to defeat Voldemort, is the ultimate consumer of the memories Dumbledore collected for the purpose of researching the history and nature of the Dark Lord.

**29. blowback**

_____ Negative consequences derived from an intelligence operation. *Example:* Voldemort's operation to get Harry to retrieve the prophecy resulted in the disclosure of Lucius Malfoy and the others as active Death Eaters.

**30. consumer**

_____ Intelligence derived from every type of intelligence available, including covert or secret intelligence. *Example:* In book 7, when trying to figure out the locations of the Horcruxes, Harry uses every source of information available to him: the information Dumbledore shared with him, articles from the *Daily Prophet*, and even Rita Skeeter's tell-all book.

# 6·4. MATCHING – GOVERNMENTAL ENTITIES IN THE POTTER SERIES

Match the Harry Potter books with the governmental entity (Department, Office, Headquarters, Committee, or Commission) that relates to the plot of that book by listing the book number that relates to the governmental entity listed.

**Book 1** – *Harry Potter and the Sorcerer's Stone* (SS 64)

**Book 2** – *Harry Potter and the Chamber of Secrets* (CS 30)

**Book 3** – *Harry Potter and the Prisoner of Azkaban* (PA 218)

**Book 4** – *Harry Potter and the Goblet of Fire* (GF 30)

**Book 5** – *Harry Potter and the Order of the Phoenix* (OP 130)

**Book 6** – *Harry Potter and the Half-Blood Prince* (HBP 9)

**Book 7** – *Harry Potter and the Deathly Hallows* (DH 209)

_____ Committee for the Disposal of Dangerous Creatures (Buckbeak)

_____ Department of Magical Games and Sports (tournament)

_____ Department of Mysteries (Harry and his friends go there)

_____ Ministry of Magic (first mentioned to Harry)

_____ Misuse of Muggle Artifacts Office (Mr. Weasley works there)

_____ Muggle-born Registration Commission ("Look out, Hermione!")

_____ Muggle Liaison Office (mentioned to the Other Prime Minister)

# 6·5. FILL IN THE BLANK – MINISTRY OF MAGIC DIRECTORY – PART 3

## Level 7

"Level seven, Department of Magical Games and
**16.** _____, incorporating the British and Irish
**17.** _____ League Headquarters, Official Gobstones
Club, and Ludicrous Patents Office" (*OP* 129).
*Hint: 16) an organized game, 17) the favorite Wizarding game.*

## Level 8

**18.** "_____ Level" – Security, Fountain of Magical
**19.** _____ (*OP* 127).
*Hint: 18) Harry has to turn in his wand here when he goes to visit
the Ministry of Magic; Wizards and Witches enter and exit from
here, and 19) I guess "sisters" don't count.*

## Level 9

"Level nine, Department of **20.**_____" (*OP* 135)
(with stairs down to the **21.**_____).
*Hint: 20) Harry retrieves the Prophecy from here, 21) the
Wizengamot holds session in one of these.*

## 6·6. WORD SEARCH – FANTASTIC BEASTS

Do your best to find all of the Fantastic Beasts.

| | | | | | | | | | |
|---|---|---|---|---|---|---|---|---|---|
| K | A | E | L | P | O | E | P | R | E | M |
| S | B | C | F | D | F | L | E | B | F | G |
| I | M | P | F | A | L | G | N | O | M | E |
| L | H | I | I | O | J | K | E | W | L | M |
| I | N | R | R | O | B | K | I | T | E | Y |
| S | Y | T | G | P | O | E | C | R | U | P |
| A | C | R | O | M | A | N | T | U | L | A |
| B | E | E | P | I | X | I | E | C | U | Q |
| R | N | D | P | S | T | F | P | K | O | N |
| Y | T | C | I | U | V | F | H | L | H | R |
| X | A | A | H | W | X | I | O | E | G | O |
| O | U | P | M | E | E | R | E | Y | N | C |
| D | R | A | G | O | N | G | N | Z | O | I |
| A | B | R | E | L | F | F | I | N | M | N |
| C | D | S | P | H | I | N | X | E | E | U |
| A | P | P | A | K | K | E | L | P | I | E |

## Find:

❑ Acromantula ❑ Boax ❑ Basilisk ❑ Bowtruckle

❑ Centaur ❑ Crup ❑ Doxy ❑ Dragon ❑ Fairy ❑ Ghoul

❑ Gnome ❑ Griffin ❑ Hippogriff ❑ Imp ❑ Kappa

❑ Kelpie ❑ Merpeople ❑ Moke ❑ Niffler ❑ Phoenix

❑ Pixie ❑ Red Cap ❑ Re'em ❑ Sphinx ❑ Tebo ❑ Troll

❑ Unicorn ❑ Yeti

**Extra Credit:** One of these words appears twice. Which one?

**Special Extra Credit:** Once you have circled all the letters, what interesting order do the remaining un-circled letters have?

## 6·7. WORD PLACEMENT – DRAGONS & SUCH

Place the dragons and other Potter terms or friends into the right "lair."

— — — — — — — — — N — — — — — —

— — — — — — — — — O — — — — — —

— — — — — — — — R — — — — —

— — — W — — — — —

— — — — — — — E — — — — — — — —

— — — — — — — G — — — —

— — — — — — — — I — — — — — —H

— — — — — — A — — — —

— — — — — — — N — — — — — — —

— — — R — — — — — —

— — — — — — — — I — — — — — —Y

— — — — — D — — — — — —

— — — G — —

— — — — — — — E — — — — — —

— — — B — — —

— — — — — — — A — — — — — — —

— — — — — — — — C — — —

— — — — — — K — — —

# PUT THESE DRAGONS OR HARRY'S FRIENDS WHERE THEY FIT:

❏ Antipodean Opaleye (17)

❏ Cedric Diggory (13)

❏ Charlie Weasley (14)

❏ Chinese Fireball (15)

❏ Common Welsh Green (16)

❏ Dragon (6)

❏ Fleur DeLacour (13)

❏ Harry Potter (11)

❏ Hebridean Black (14)

❏ Hungarian Horntail (17)

❏ Norbert (7)

❏ Peruvian Vipertooth (18)

❏ Romanian Longhorn (16)

❏ Rubius Hagrid (12)

❏ Swedish Short-Snout (17)

❏ Triwizard (9)

❏ Ukrainian Ironbelly (18)

❏ Victor Krum (10)

# CHAPTER 6

# ANSWERS

## 6·1. ANSWERS TO PASSWORDS TO GET INTO HEADMASTER'S TOWER

**Password 15 – Lemon drop** (*CS* 204)
**Password 16 – Cockroach Cluster** (*GF* 579)
**Password 17 – Acid Pops** (*HBP* 181, 196)
**Password 18 – toffee éclairs** (*HBP* 493)
**Password 19 – Dumbledore** (*DH* 662)


## 6·2. ANSWERS TO BREAKING THE CODE – PASSWORDS FOR OTHER PLACES OR POTTERWATCH

**Passwords to Get Into Slytherin Tower**
**Password 20 – pure-blood** (*CS* 221)
**Passwords to Get Into Prefects' Bathroom**
**Password 21 – pine fresh** (*GF* 431, 459)
**Passwords to Listen to Potterwatch**
**Password 22 – Albus** (*DH* 438)
**Password 23 – Mad-Eye** (*DH* 444)


## 6·3. ANSWERS TO MATCHING – SPY TERMS IN THE HARRY POTTER SERIES FOR HOGWARTS ALUMNAE

**30 consumer, 29 blowback, and 28 all-source intelligence**

# 6·4. ANSWERS TO MATCHING – GOVERNMENTAL ENTITIES IN THE POTTER SERIES:

**Book 1 – *Harry Potter and the Sorcerer's Stone* (*SS* 64)**

**Book 2 – *Harry Potter and the Chamber of Secrets* (*CS* 30)**

**Book 3 – *Harry Potter and the Prisoner of Azkaban* (*PA* 218)**

**Book 4 – *Harry Potter and the Goblet of Fire* (*GF* 30)**

**Book 5 – *Harry Potter and the Order of the Phoenix* (*OP* 130)**

**Book 6 – *Harry Potter and the Half-Blood Prince* (*HBP* 9)**

**Book 7 – *Harry Potter and the Deathly Hallows* (*DH* 209)**

_____ 3 _____ Committee for the Disposal of Dangerous Creatures (Buckbeak)

_____ 4 _____ Department of Magical Games and Sports (tournament)

_____ 5 _____ Department of Mysteries (Harry and his friends go there)

_____ 1 _____ Ministry of Magic (first mentioned to Harry)

_____ 2 _____ Misuse of Muggle Artifacts Office (Mr. Weasley works there)

_____7_____ Muggle-born Registration Commission ("Look out, Hermione!")

_____6_____ Muggle Liaison Office (mentioned to the Other Prime Minister)

# 6.5. ANSWERS TO FILL IN THE BLANK – MINISTRY OF MAGIC DIRECTORY – PART 3

**16.** Department of Magical Games and **Sports**

**17.** British and Irish **Quidditch** League Headquarters

**18.** **Atrium** Level

**19.** Fountain of Magical **Brothers**

**20.** Department of **Mysteries**

**21.** stairs down to the **courtrooms**

## 6·6. ANSWERS TO WORD SEARCH – FANTASTIC BEASTS

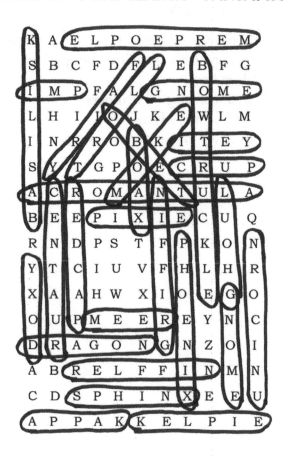

Extra Credit: One of these words appears twice. Which one?
**Gnome**.

Special Extra Credit: once you have circled all the letters, what interesting order do the remaining un-circled letters have?
**The alphabet in order, A to Z, and then A to E.**

# 6·7. WORD PLACEMENT – DRAGONS & SUCH

Place the dragons and other Potter terms or friends into the right "lair."

ANTIPODEA**N**OPALEYE

SWEDISH SH**O**RT-SNOUT

CHINESE FI**R**EBALL

TRI**W**IZARD

COMMON **W**ELSH GREEN

CEDRIC DI**G**GORY

PERUVIAN V**I**PERTOOT**H**

RUBIUS H**A**GRID

HUNGARIA**N** HORNTAIL

HAR**R**Y POTTER

UKRAINIAN **I**RONBELL**Y**

HEBRI**D**EAN BLACK

DRA**G**ON

CHARLI**E** WEASLEY

NOR**B**ERT

ROMANI**A**N LONGHORN

FLEUR DELA**C**OUR

VICTOR **K**RUM

# BACKFLAP. ANSWERS TO FILL IN THE BLANK – THE POTTER SERIES FAMILY TREE – POTTERS, DURSLEYS, WEASLEYS, AND LUPINS*

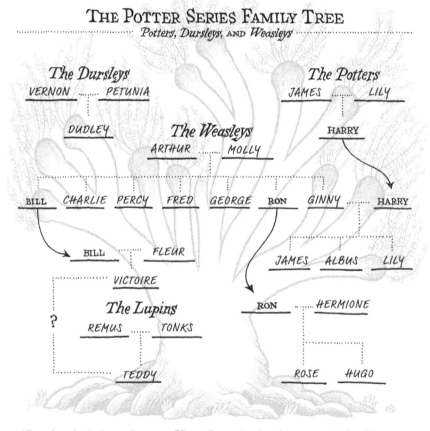

THE POTTER SERIES FAMILY TREE
Potters, Dursleys, AND Weasleys

The Dursleys
VERNON ....... PETUNIA

The Potters
JAMES ....... LILY

DUDLEY

The Weasleys
ARTHUR ....... MOLLY

HARRY

BILL   CHARLIE   PERCY   FRED   GEORGE   RON   GINNY ....... HARRY

BILL ....... FLEUR

JAMES   ALBUS   LILY

VICTOIRE

The Lupins
?   REMUS ....... TONKS

RON ....... HERMIONE

TEDDY

ROSE   HUGO

*Based exclusively on the seven Harry Potter books; does not include additions by J. K. Rowling outside the seven books, such as Bill and Fleur's other two children Dominque and Louis, Percy and Audrey's children Molly and Lucy, George and Angelina (Johnson)'s children Fred and Roxanne, or Luna and Rolf Scamander twin sons Lorcan and Lysander. We also do not include Lucius or Narcissa Malfoy, or their son Draco, his wife Astoria, or their son Scorpius.

# THE INTELLIGENCE CYCLE

The intelligence cycle is the organized system by which a country gathers and uses intelligence information. Before the cycle begins, however, there must be some important purpose for gathering the target information. It is not practical to collect every possible bit of information on every subject—the result would be an overwhelming flood. Instead, intelligence organizations identify the information that is most essential to its goals and the ways it will be used to determine government policy—before sending someone to retrieve it.

Generally speaking, most intelligence entities follow the same steps, known as the intelligence cycle. Most of the work that people think of as "spying" takes place in just one step, Collection. But even the most important secret isn't worth much without a way to retrieve it, ways of verifying that it is accurate information, and a plan to make use of it. The steps of the intelligence cycle are:

1. **Planning and direction:** Members of the senior intelligence staff identify important issues and the types of information that are most important to obtain.

2. **Collection:** Case officers and analysts collect all possible information on the target subject,

including open source information, intelligence from case officers and their agents, and data from spy satellites, surveillance, wiretapping, intercepted communications, and other sources.

3. **Processing:** Trained professionals review and organize the collected data. This might include translating information from foreign-language sources into English, creating databases to combine information from many sources, scanning images such as maps and photographs, and other tasks to prepare the information for analysis.

4. **Analysis:** Once the information is organized, analysts comb through every detail, checking facts and comparing the various sources to other sources in search of hidden patterns or clues. In addition, they compare the new data with older information already in the organization's possession. The goal of analysis is to identify the most correct bits of intelligence and assemble them into the most accurate possible picture of the plans and resources of the target country or organization.

5. **Production:** The results of the analysis step are assembled into a clear and accurate report, called a *product,* that can be used by the decision maker or department that requested the intelligence. There are many types of products, everything from general reports on the history of a country to detailed

investigations into the military capabilities of a particular adversary.

6.  **Dissemination:** The intelligence product is distributed to the person or people who need it to make decisions. The best-known intelligence product is the President's Daily Brief, a report that is distributed to the president of the United States, the vice president, the Joint Chiefs of Staff, and those selected by the President to see it.

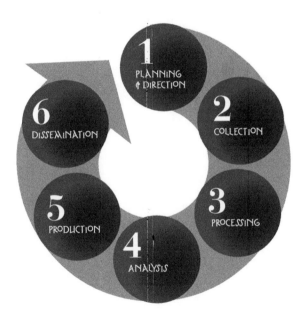

# TYPES OF INTELLIGENCE

**Geospatial intelligence (GEOINT)** Information obtained from images of physical spaces, such as maps, satellite images (IMINT, or imagery intelligence), and photographs (PHOINT, or photographic intelligence).

**Human intelligence (HUMINT)** Information obtained directly from individuals—either our own spies or some other person who is on the ground in a particular country and willing to provide us with important information.

**Measurement and signature intelligence (MASINT)** Information obtained by remote sensing technologies such as radar and sonar.

**Open source intelligence (OSINT)** Information that is available to anybody, such as newspapers, public websites, television and radio broadcasts, speeches, press releases, and government publications.

**Signals intelligence (SIGINT)** Information obtained by intercepting signals. This combines earlier types of intelligence, including communications intelligence (COMINT, communications between people, such as telephone and radio communication) and electronic intelligence (ELINT, electronic signals such as the waves emitted by particular weapons and machines), and any other information collected by electronic devices or technologies.

# GLOSSARY

**access:** Authorization to receive information that is limited to a select group of people who have the correct security clearance. *Example:* Members of the Order of the Phoenix attend the meetings at number twelve, Grimmauld Place, but Harry and his friends are not allowed to attend the meetings because of their age and not yet being members of the Order of the Phoenix.

**agent:** An individual who is hired or employed by a country, or is acting on his or her own, to spy or obtain inside information; that information may be given or sold to a country or another entity. *Example:* Professor Quirrell and Peter Pettigrew both serve as agents for Voldemort, assisting him in regaining his corporeal body.

**agent provocateur:** An individual who serves as a catalyst to get others to take actions. *Example:* Lee Jordan is trying to provoke Professor Umbridge by placing nifflers in her office.

**all-source intelligence:** Intelligence derived from every type of intelligence available, including covert or secret intelligence. *Example:* In book 7, when trying to figure out the locations of the Horcruxes, Harry uses every source of information available to him: the information Dumbledore shared with him, articles from the Daily Prophet, and even Rita Skeeter's tell-all book.

**analysis:** The use of logic and observation to reach conclusions that are correct and based on fact. *Example:* In book 7, Harry, Hermione, and Ron use analysis to determine where the Horcruxes are located.

**asset:** Something of value. In the spy world, an asset is normally a high-ranking individual or important person who is being protected or providing information. *Example:* Each time Harry is moved from number four, Privet Drive, members of the Order of the Phoenix form a security team to protect him because he is a high-value asset.

**background check:** An exceedingly thorough review of a person's history; in the world of espionage, a background check usually involves an investigator meeting with hundreds of the subject's personal and professional contacts. *Example:* In book 6, Dumbledore does a thorough background check on Tom Riddle, researching and interviewing anyone who has had contact with, or information about, Tom Riddle.

**bias:** An inclination, not necessarily based on facts or sound reasoning, toward or against a particular person or group. *Example:* Professor Umbridge has a bias against half-breeds, which comes to light (much to her eventual dismay) in her discussions with the centaurs.

**black bag job:** A surreptitious or covert entry into a home, office, or other location without the knowledge of the owner. The term originates from the need to bring a black bag full of tools by which to gain entry, such as lock-picking tools. A black bag job is successful when the person gains entry, obtains the information desired or places surveillance devices, and leaves undetected and without the knowledge of the person who works or lives there. *Example:* Harry's first covert visit to Professor Umbridge's office to talk to Sirius is a successful (though not perfect) black bag job.

**blackmail:** Using information about someone to force or coerce them to do something for you. *Example:* By threatening to disclose Rita Skeeter as an unregistered Animagus, Hermione blackmails the reporter into writing a true article about what happened to Harry at the end of the Triwizard Tournament when Voldemort returned.

**blow back:** Negative consequences derived from an intelligence operation or false information distributed by an intelligence agency. *Example:* Voldemort's operation to get Harry to retrieve the prophecy results in the disclosure of Lucius Malfoy and the others as active Death Eaters.

**bribe:** An offer of money or other valuable inducement to convince the recipient to do what the offerer wants. *Example:* Draco Malfoy implies that his father, Lucius, has "bribed" Cornelius Fudge and the Ministry of Magic by providing money and information to influence the Ministry's decisions.

**bug:** An electronic surveillance device that can intercept phone calls and other communications, or that can transmit sounds from the bugged room. A common device consists of a microphone attached to a tiny radio frequency transmitter that broadcasts all noise in the room to the spy's receiver. *Example:* Wizards don't necessarily need surveillance devices. Animagus Rita Skeeter, in her beetle form, can sneak into a room and overhear private conversations—literally "bugging" a room!

**case officer:** An intelligence officer assigned to spy or recruit agents. *Example:* When Harry uses his Invisibility Cloak to get into the restricted section of the Hogwarts library, he is acting alone as a spy, and as a case officer.

**cell:** A group that is working together on a combined project or mission. *Example:* Dumbledore's Army is a group of students assembled to practice Defense Against the Dark Arts.

**Central Intelligence Agency (CIA):** The primary human source intelligence service of the United States for gathering intelligence abroad.

**classified information:** Generally speaking, information that is restricted to a small number of people who have the correct clearance to access it. The levels of classification are, from least to greatest restriction, Confidential, Classified, Secret, Top Secret, and Sensitive Compartmented Information. *Example:* In book 1, Hagrid mentions that his trip to Gringotts to retrieve an item from Vault No. 713 is "Hogwarts business" (SS 74). The information is secret, but not so highly restricted that the business cannot be conducted in public during work hours.

**clearance:** The level of access a person is authorized to have to confidential or secured information; levels include Confidential, Classified, Secret, Top Secret, and Sensitive Compartmented Information (code-word clearance required). *Example:* When Harry asks what had been in Vault 713, Hagrid refuses to tell Harry and his friends because they don't have clearance for "Very secret, Hogwarts business" (*SS* 74).

**code breaking:** The art of taking a message and extrapolating its content. *Example:* The inscription on the Mirror of Erised, "Erised stra ehru oyt ube cafru oyt on wohsi" (SS 207), is actually a single sentence in English.

**coded message:** Information disguised so that only its intended recipient can read or understand it. *Example:* The writing on the Mirror of Erised is written in code: the inscription, "Erised stra ehru oyt ube cafru oyt on wohsi" (*SS* 207), has been encoded by being written backwards and re-spaced. The true message reads, "I show not your face but your heart's desire."

**code name:** An alternative name for a person or thing that is known only to a limited number of people. *Example:* When Harry writes to his godfather, Sirius, he refers to him as Snuffles (OP 280).

**concealment:** The act of hiding something, often in plain sight. *Example:* Harry's Invisibility Cloak assists him on numerous occasions in not being seen.

**consumer:** The person or entity receiving intelligence information, such as a head of state or other senior official with decisionmaking authority. *Example:* Harry Potter, as the person destined to defeat Voldemort, is the ultimate consumer of the memories Dumbledore collected for the purpose of researching the history and nature of the Dark Lord.

**counterintelligence:** The use of intelligence or special devices to prevent someone from spying on you. *Example:* In book 7, Hermione casts many spells and enchantments around their tent to prevent their discovery when they are on the run.

**countermeasures:** Acts or devices that prevent someone from observing a spy's activities. *Example:* In order to prevent the children from listening in on the Order of the Phoenix's meetings with Extendable Ears, Mrs. Weasley employs countermeasures (an Imperturbable Charm) on the door.

**courier:** A person who transfers a message from an agent to some other person or to headquarters. *Example:* Throughout the Harry Potter series, owls are used to send messages.

**cover story:** A false story that conceals a person's true reasons for being in a particular place. *Example:* The Dursleys tell their neighbors that Harry is gone during the school year because he is attending St. Brutus's Secure Center for Incurably Criminal Boys.

**deep cover:** A mission or assignment so secret that only one or two people know of its existence. *Example:* No one knows about Snape's role spying on Voldemort, except Dumbledore.

**disguise:** A change of apparel or appearance that makes a person unrecognizable. *Example:* Barty Crouch Jr., through the use of Polyjuice Potion, appears to be Professor Alastor Moody.

**disinformation:** Intentionally incorrect information, often provided to an adversary for the purpose of influencing the adversary's reactions. *Example:* Hermione, when captured by Umbridge and the members of the Inquisitorial Squad, lies about hiding Dumbledore's secret weapon in the Forbidden Forest; as a result, Umbridge takes Harry and Hermione to the forest, where they are able to escape, thanks to the centaurs and Grawp.

**diversion:** An occurrence that results in a person shifting attention away from the immediate situation or going elsewhere. *Example:* In order to assist Harry in getting into Professor Umbridge's office the first time, the Weasley twins use fireworks to get Umbridge away from her office.

**double agent:** An agent employed by one entity but working in reality for another entity or person. *Example:* Snape is a double agent who is working for Dumbledore and spying on Voldemort, who thinks Snape is his agent!

**eavesdropping:** Surreptitiously listening to someone's conversation. *Example:* As a young Death Eater, Snape listens in on Dumbledore as he meets with Sybill Trelawney and overhears the first part of the prophecy, which he reports to Voldemort.

**eyes-only communication:** Information that is so important that it can only be shown to the recipient—usually the leader of a country—and not left in that person's possession in the form of a paper or electronic copy. *Example:* Dumbledore shows Harry the memories he has collected in the Pensieve; the memories have not been transcribed or copied, making them more secure.

**Federal Bureau of Investigation (FBI):** The primary domestic law enforcement agency of the United States government; it investigates all potentially illegal activities that occur in the United States, including acts of espionage by foreign governments on U.S. soil.

**handler:** A senior intelligence officer in charge of an agent. *Example:* Dumbledore gives Snape assignments regarding his spying on Voldemort.

**headquarters:** The main location of an intelligence organization. *Example:* Number twelve, Grimmauld Place, is the headquarters for the Order of the Phoenix.

**informant:** A person who provides inside information to someone else. *Example:* Marietta, Cho's friend, tells Professor Umbridge about the secret meetings of Dumbledore's Army.

**inside information:** Knowledge gleaned by a person already in or placed inside an organization for purposes of spying on that organization. *Example:* Kingsley Shacklebolt, while supposedly looking for Sirius, is actually gathering inside information from the Ministry for the Order of the Phoenix.

**intelligence:** Information or communication that can be evaluated and used to determine facts, intentions, and capabilities of an adversary, generally organized within an intellectual framework that can be thoroughly analyzed. *Example:* Arthur Weasley uses his job at the Ministry of Magic to collect intelligence about Death Eaters' activities and the Ministry's own plans.

**interrogation:** A lengthy questioning of a person, usually by an authoritarian figure, such as a police officer or detective. *Example:* At Harry's hearing, Cornelius Fudge asks Harry questions to get answers that Fudge wants to use against him.

**lookout:** A person assigned to warn others if someone approaches during a covert operation. *Example:* Ginny and Luna serve as lookouts when Harry sneaks into Professor Umbridge's office the second time.

**mole:** A person stationed inside a government or spy agency who regularly provides information to another government or spy agency. *Example:* Unbeknownst to the "other" Prime Minister, his new assistant, Kingsley Shacklebolt, is actually a government mole for the Ministry of Magic.

**National Security Agency (NSA):** The U.S. agency charged with intercepting and gathering phone and electronic communications from persons and countries of interest.

**observation:** The process of looking at a place, person, or situation and, importantly, remembering the sights accurately. A skilled intelligence officer will have extensive training in gathering visual information. *Example:* When Harry and his friends enter the kitchen after a meeting of the Order of the Phoenix, Harry observes on the table plans for a building—and later correctly surmises that the plans are for the Ministry of Magic.

**open source intelligence:** Information that is generally open to all, such as newspapers, maps, websites, and other public documents. *Example:* The *Daily Prophet* is an open source that provides Harry and his friends with substantial amounts of information, even when it is asserting false facts or conclusions.

**password:** A word or number sequence that allows access to a building or information. *Example:* In order to get into Dumbledore's office, both the students and the teachers must use a password.

**polygraph:** A real-world lie-detecting device used to measure extremely small physical reactions of a person while answering preplanned and very precise questions. It is used extensively in the security world, but not yet considered reliable enough to be admitted automatically into court proceedings. *Example:* The Sneakoscope, which senses when someone is doing something untrustworthy in its vicinity, acts as a polygraph in the Wizarding world.

**psychological assessment:** The use of information about a person's traits, characteristics, background, and psychological makeup to predict that person's reactions or future actions. *Example:* Voldemort, knowing Harry's tendency to play the hero, lays a trap and convinces Harry (through information implanted in his dreams) that Sirius has been captured and is being tortured in the Department of Mysteries.

**recruiting:** The process of getting someone to join your side. *Example:* Harry convinces Kreacher to work for him by offering him respect and the chance to protect a Black family heirloom.

**safe house:** A place where agents or defectors can be safely hidden; often a place to debrief agents. *Example:* Number twelve, Grimmauld Place, is used as a safe house by the Order of the Phoenix throughout the last half of the series—until it is compromised.

**secure communication:** A means of communication that is safe from eavesdropping or observation. *Example:* Harry uses Professor

Umbridge's fireplace to communicate with Sirius because it is not being monitored by his enemies.

**security detail:** A group of people assigned to protect an important person. *Example:* Harry, when he is taken from the Dursleys' home at the beginning of each school term, often has a security detail to protect and transport him.

**sensitive compartmented information facility (SCIF):** A secure facility from which people with the proper security clearance may retrieve and submit extremely sensitive information, often located in a vault or place with limited access and proper security protection and countermeasures.

**signal:** Any subtle action conveying a covert message or indication to take a preplanned action. *Example:* When Harry is being taken from Privet Drive by his security team in book 5, someone is assigned to send up sparks into the air to indicate that it is safe to proceed.

**situational awareness:** A person's intentional attentiveness to what is going on around him or her, especially in an area known to be dangerous. *Example:* When Harry, Ron, and Hermione sneak into the Ministry to get the locket from Umbridge, they are aware that they are in enemy territory and pay attention to every detail to find their way while remaining undetected.

**sleeper agent:** An agent left for an extended period, sometimes even years, awaiting a particular assignment or a signal indicating that the time has come to execute a preplanned mission. *Example:* Mrs. Figg is a sleeper agent assigned by Dumbledore to watch over Harry and act only if the circumstances warrant it, such as when she intercedes after Harry and Dudley are attacked by Dementors.

**source:** Any person who provides information to an intelligence officer. *Example:* Rookwood acts as a source when he informs Voldemort that he used to work at the Ministry of Magic's Department of

Mysteries and reveals that Avery should have known that Bode could not have retrieved the prophecy.

**spycraft:** Often called tradecraft, all operational aspects and techniques used in spying, including the use of psychology, weapons, intelligence, analysis, secure locations, indirect communication, forgery, and disguises. *Example:* Harry practices spycraft throughout the series, such as when he eavesdrops on his uncle, conceals himself under the Invisibility Cloak, breaks into Professor Umbridge's office, and maintains equanimity even under great pressure.

**surveillance:** The systematic observation of a chosen target. *Example:* When Harry, Ron, and Hermione are in hiding at number twelve, Grimmauld Place, they notice they are under surveillance by Death Eaters outside, who are waiting and watching for a sign of anyone going inside the building.

**turning:** Convincing an agent to switch sides. *Example:* Dumbledore turns Snape when he agrees to protect Lily Potter from Voldemort and Snape agrees, in return, to "Anything" (DH 678).

**walk-in:** A person who voluntarily agrees to provide information to an intelligence officer or agency, usually after literally walking into an embassy or otherwise offering his or her services. *Example:* Snape, when he asks Dumbledore to protect and save Lily Potter, is a walk-in.

# SELECTED BIBLIOGRAPHY

Allen, Thomas B. *Declassified: 50 Top-Secret Documents that Changed History*. Washington, D.C.: National Geographic, 2008. (Forward by Peter Earnest.).

Boughey, Lynn. *Mission to Chara*. Minot, ND: North American Heritage Press, 2000.

Boughey, Lynn and Peter Earnest. *Harry Potter and the Art of Spying*. Minneapolis: Wise Ink Creative Publishing, 2014.

Earnest, Peter and Suzanne Harper. *The Real Spy's Guide to Becoming a Spy*. New York: Abrams Books for Young Readers, 2009.

Earnest, Peter and Maryann Karinch. *Business Confidential: Lessons for Corporate Success from Inside the CIA*. New York: AMACOM, 2011.

Rowling, J. K. *Harry Potter and the Sorcerer's Stone*. New York: Scholastic, 1998.

_____. *Harry Potter and the Chamber of Secrets*. New York: Scholastic, 1999.

_____. *Harry Potter and the Prisoner of Azkaban*. New York: Scholastic, 1999.

_____. *Harry Potter and the Goblet of Fire*. New York: Scholastic, 2000.

_____. *Harry Potter and the Order of the Phoenix*. New York: Scholastic, 2003.

_____. *Harry Potter and the Half-Blood Prince.* New York: Scholastic, 2005.

_____. *Harry Potter and the Deathly Hallows.* New York: Scholastic, 2007.

Weiser, Benjamin. *A Secret Life: The Polish Officer, His Covert Mission, and the Price He Paid to Save His Country.* New York: Public Affairs/Perseus Group, 2004.

# ABOUT THE AUTHORS AND ILLUSTRATOR

**Lynn Boughey** is a lawyer with more than thirty years of practice in North Dakota. Lynn's love of books and reading began at a very young age, and continues to this day. Lynn is North Dakota's first Truman Scholar, a Congressional scholarship begun in 1977. A graduate of Grinnell College and Hamline University School of Law *cum laude*, Lynn also taught at the college level for over sixteen years, primarily in the areas of political science, international studies, criminal law and procedure, and terrorism. Author of *Mission to Chara*, a spy novel published in 2000, Lynn is presently working on a three-part murder-mystery legal thriller, *Murder at the Second Constitutional Convention*. Lynn is a member of the Association of Former Intelligence Officers (AFIO) and the Defense Orientation Conference Association (DOCA). Lynn continues to practice law in North Dakota and lives in Montana with his fourteen-year-old twin daughters.

**Peter Earnest** has served as the Founding Executive Director of the International Spy Museum since it opened in 2002. Born in Edinburgh, Scotland, his father was an American vice-consul and his mother, an English woman of Irish background. As a young boy Peter loved performing magic and he continues his life-long interest in magic and magicians. Following graduation from Georgetown University in Washington, D.C. and a stint in the Marines, Peter began his thirty-six-year CIA career, which included more than twenty-five years in the agency's Clandestine Service. A member of the CIA's Senior Intelligence Service, he was awarded the agency's Intelligence Medal of Merit for superior performance throughout his career. In his final posting, Peter also served as the agency's principal spokesman, working to share information more openly with the media and the public. After retiring, Peter served as President and Chairman of the Board of Directors of the Association of Former Intelligence Officers (AFIO). Frequently inter-viewed by the media, he is also the author of several books relating to tradecraft, including *The Real Spy's Guide to Becoming a Spy* and *Business Confidential: Lessons for Corporate Success from Inside the CIA*. He is married to Karen Rice, has four daughters, and lives in McLean, Virginia.

**Kevin Cannon** is a well-known Minneapolis illustrator and cartoonist. He has written and illustrated many graphic novels, including an arctic adventure tale called *Far Arden*. Kevin grew up in St. Louis Park, a suburb of Minneapolis, where at the age of three he began his "career" as an illustrator drawing with markers on foam board. He was asked by friends and teachers to do many illustrations throughout high school, including program covers and sports T-shirts. Kevin attended Grinnell College and found his calling doing a comic strip for the college newspaper. These days his favorite things to draw are cartoon adventure maps, so it's no surprise that his favorite part about the Harry Potter series is the Marauder's Map.

# NOTES